Wisdom of the Tao Te Ching

The Code of a Spiritual Warrior

BY

ASHOK KUMAR MALHOTRA

State University of New York, Oneonta

Copyright ©2013 by *Ashok Kumar Malhotra*

All rights reserved. No portion of this publication may be duplicated in any way without the expressed written consent of the author, except in the form of brief excerpts or quotations for the purpose of review.

10 9 8 7 6 5 4 3 2 1

ISBN 978-0-9829141-2-0

Library of Congress Cataloging-in-Publication Data

Title: **Wisdom of the Tao Te Ching**
The Code of a Spiritual Warrior
Author: Ashok Kumar Malhotra
Subject: Philosophy, Meditation, Mysticism, Spirituality, Art of Living, Wisdom, Art of Warfare and Government

Cover by author — Male-Female: Inseparable Yet Unique
Pictures in the book — Courtesy of Linda Drake

In the 2nd edition of Wisdom of the Tao Te Ching, the text remains unchanged while photographs are added.

This edition is printed by The Village Printer of Oneonta, NY.

The Tao Te Ching, signifying the
"Way and Its Power," is for me the
"genuine love expressing itself
through compassionate service of
the down-trodden of the humanity."

Linda Marie Drake

is the quintessence of this sentiment.
I dedicate this work to her so
that she will never stop helping
the unfortunate people of this planet.

CONTENTS

Preface ix

Foreword xx

Introduction xxvi

The Transcreated Text of the Tao Te Ching 1

Book One (Chapters 1-37)

Chapter 1 - The Tao 5
Chapter 2 - Contraries 7
Chapter 3 - Going with the Flow 9
Chapter 4 - The Mysterious Tao 11
Chapter 5 - Tao and Sage 13
Chapter 6 - The Great Mother 15
Chapter 7 - Compassion for Others 17
Chapter 8 - Highest Good is Like Water 19
Chapter 9 - Step Back 21
Chapter 10 - Nature of the Inner Power 23
Chapter 11 - Usefulness of Emptiness 25
Chapter 12 - Sense versus Inner Vision 27
Chapter 13 - Oppositions 29
Chapter 14 - The Ineffable Tao 31

-v-

CONTENTS

Chapter 15 - Wise Sages *33*
Chapter 16 - The Source *35*
Chapter 17 - Who is the Best Leader? *37*
Chapter 18 - Forgetfulness of the Tao *39*
Chapter 19 - Simplicity *41*
Chapter 20 - Nourished by the Great Mother *43*
Chapter 21 - Mark of the Tao *45*
Chapter 22 - Overcome Through Yielding *47*
Chapter 23 - Merging into the Tao *49*
Chapter 24 - What the Sage Avoids? *51*
Chapter 25 - Nature of the Tao *53*
Chapter 26 - Contrasts *55*
Chapter 27 - Wondrous Secret *57*
Chapter 28 - The Force Within (Te) *59*
Chapter 29 - Avoiding Extremes *61*
Chapter 30 - Use of Force *63*
Chapter 31 - Evil of Weapons *65*
Chapter 32 - The Indescribable Tao *67*
Chapter 33 - To Die Without Perishing *69*
Chapter 34 - The Great Tao *71*
Chapter 35 - The Inexhaustible Tao *73*
Chapter 36 - Perception of Things *75*
Chapter 37 - By Doing Nothing, Everything is Done *77*

Book Two (Chapters 38-81)

Chapter 38 - Inner Force (Te) *81*
Chapter 39 - Tao Connection *83*
Chapter 40 - The Way *85*
Chapter 41 - Hearers of the Tao *87*
Chapter 42 - Male and Female *89*
Chapter 43 - Action of Non-Action *91*

CONTENTS

Chapter 44 - To Be Fulfilled 93
Chapter 45 - Let the Tao Work! 95
Chapter 46 - Secret of Contentment 97
Chapter 47 - The Nature of inaction 99
Chapter 48 - Let things Be 101
Chapter 49 - The Sage as a Little Child 103
Chapter 50 - Living a Deathless Life 105
Chapter 51 - Tao and Te 107
Chapter 52 - The Eternal Mother 109
Chapter 53 - Going Against the Way 111
Chapter 54 - Nature of Te 113
Chapter 55 - Te and the Child 115
Chapter 56 - Highest Human Being 117
Chapter 57 - Non-Doing (Wu Wei) 119
Chapter 58 - Government and People 121
Chapter 59 - Moderation 123
Chapter 60 - Frying a Small Fish 125
Chapter 61 - Large and Small Countries 127
Chapter 62 - The Love of Tao 129
Chapter 63 - Easy and Difficult 131
Chapter 64 - Haste Makes Waste 133
Chapter 65 - Harmony 135
Chapter 66 - Humility 137
Chapter 67 - Three Gems 139
Chapter 68 - Non-Competition 141
Chapter 69 - The Underdog 143
Chapter 70 - Simple Teaching 145
Chapter 71 - Know by Knowing Nothing 147
Chapter 72 - The Force 149
Chapter 73 - Tao's Web 151

CONTENTS

Chapter 74 - Death *153*
Chapter 75 - Government *155*
Chapter 76 - Life and Death *157*
Chapter 77 - Balance *159*
Chapter 78 - Paradoxical Truth *161*
Chapter 79 - Good Men *163*
Chapter 80 - Ideal Life *165*
Chapter 81 - Pure Action *167*

Afterword *169*

Bibliography *185*

PREFACE

Wisdom of the Tao Te Ching
Douglas W. Shrader
Distinguished Teaching Professor
& Chair, Philosophy Department
SUNY Oneonta

A Beginning or Two

The origins of the Tao Te Ching are shrouded in mystery. Legend has it that the book was composed by a Chinese sage known as "Lao tzu" (circa 600 BC). According to one popular account, Lao tzu was stopped at the western border of the kingdom by a seemingly ordinary guard. Fortunately, this was not your stereotypical gruff, ignorant border guard who searched travelers for jade and other material objects considered precious by his society, but rather an exceptional man who had the presence of mind to realize that Lao tzu was leaving the country with something of far greater value: timeless insight and understanding concerning human nature as well as the world in which we live. He prevailed upon the traveler to jot down the essential elements of his wisdom in a sort, pithy book known to generations of Chinese as "The Lao tzu" (i.e. the book written by Lao tzu). It is now known to the world at large as "The Tao Te Ching" (roughly, "The Way/Power of the Tao and the Te").

The tale of the border guard who sees what others miss is a lovely story, but many contemporary scholars regard it as just that: a story. Textual and historical evidence, they argue, suggests that the text was composed over a period of

PREFACE

years – perhaps even several hundred years – by an unidentified assortment of authors. For scholars, the difference in these two accounts is profoundly significant. The first presupposed a virtual god-man, a singular sage who reluctantly shared a small portion of his knowledge with a world he was leaving behind: a world that did not – and perhaps even still cannot – understand more than a tiny fraction of the wisdom contained in the pages of the text. The second account makes a very different set of assumptions: namely, that there was an ongoing community of scholars who discussed and debated the principal issues of the text over a period of time, gradually working out a reasonably consistent set of answers to questions about human nature (the social and/or political world in which we make our lives), relationships between humans and nonhumans (the so-called "natural world" in which we are immersed), and even relationships between each of these and a more fundamental/basic/all-pervading yet paradoxically elusive "reality" known variously as "Tao" or "Te".

Even Lao tzu himself is a figure shrouded in mystery. One legend claims that he was already an old man when he was born (bearded, wizened, etc.). The term "Lao tzu" (also rendered "Laozi") means roughly "ancient, revered teacher" and thus is not likely to be a proper name, but rather an honorific title used by his students. Not surprisingly, some scholars have come to question the existence of Lao tzu as a singular, historical individual, choosing to treat him instead as a composite of the many different sages who

PREFACE

pondered the Tao and composed the various segments of the Tao Te Ching over a protracted period of time.

This sense of mystery, this lack of historical certitude and categorical assurance, may be disconcerting to some. If so, this is an appropriate text for you to ponder, for one of the central lessons of the Tao Te Ching concerns the human tendency to classify everything we encounter as "this" rather than "that". The Tao, it teaches, is beyond this type of dichotomous pigeonholing. The restrictions of either-or and us-them logic limit, not the Tao, but rather the hearts and minds of those who are confused and unenlightened. To embrace the Tao and live a richer, more authentic and more satisfying life, we must be willing to leave behind (or at least set aside) a series of assumptions about ourselves as well as the world(s) in which we live.

The Author and the Audience

Dr. Ashok Malhotra is a critically acclaimed author who has published books in Existentialism and Asian Philosophy, as well as translations of two classic texts of India: the Bhagavagita (Prentice Hall, 1999) and the Yoga Sutras of Patanjali (Ashgate, 2001). Because he is also an uncommonly conscientious and gifted teacher, he has been named a "Distinguished Teaching Professor" by the State University of New York (the highest rank available, awarded only to a select few following extensive review and recommendation by the Chancellor to the Board of Trustees). As such, he approaches a text like the Tao Te

PREFACE

Ching with a dual perspective cultivated over a lifetime of intellectual inquiry and human exchange: he combines the critical, scholarly, and insightful mind of a philosopher with the patient, skillful, and experienced heart of a true teacher. The result is a product that Dr. Malhotra likes to call a "transcreation." Instead of focusing on a "translation" of the words from one language to another, he labors to find a clear, easy-to-understand way of expressing the meaning. Hence the title of this text: "Wisdom of the Tao Te Ching: The Code of a Spiritual Warrior." As Dr. Ronnie Littlejohn indicates in his [preface], Dr. Malhotra's "transcreation" is not only more accessible than many alternative translations, but conveys the vitality of the text in a way that often gets lost in the process of trying to render a strict linguistic equivalent.

The Chinese term rendered "Tao" or "Dao" is pronounced with a sound somewhere between the two alternative spellings: i.e. with an initial sound somewhere between a "T" and a "D" followed by "ow" (as in "how now brown cow"). In similar manner, "Te" is sometimes rendered "De" (pronounced somewhere between "duh" and "day") and "Ching" many be expressed as "jing" (as in "Jingle Bells"). In recent years, the People's Republic of China and many scholars (e.g. Dr. Littlejohn) have come to prefer "Daodejing" to "Tao Te Ching". Thus in creating the present "transcreation," Dr. Malhotra was faced with a choice. Should he use the linguistic form popular with contemporary scholars (Daodejing) or the one most readily recognized by ordinary Americans (Tao Te Ching)? For Dr.

PREFACE

Malhotra, the choice was obvious; for his goal was not to impress other scholars, but rather to make the text accessible to college students as well as the general public. Moreover, in the final analysis, the choice between "Tao" and "Dao" is at best arbitrary and incomplete: neither corresponds directly to the Chinese symbol it attempts to represent. In fact, as expressed in the opening line of the Tao Te Ching (Chapter 1), even the Chinese symbol fails to correspond to the true Tao!

Because Dr. Malhotra has used ordinary, easy-to-understand language, Wisdom of the Tao Te Ching: The Code of a Spiritual Warrior is an ideal book for beginners. You do not need a background in either Philosophy or Chinese Studies to access the wisdom of the Tao. It is also a useful book for intermediary students who have already encountered the Tao Te Ching in another translation, for passages that seem abstruse or impenetrable in other formulations spring to life in Dr. Malhotra's capable hands. Finally, the text will also appeal to advanced students and professional scholars: even those who believe they have grasped the "deep, underlying meaning" of the Tao Te Ching will be forced to reexamine the linguistic and metaphysical foundations of their interpretations.

How to Read the Tao Te Ching

Because many of the chapters are extremely short, most people can read through the entire text in less than an hour. While there is much that you will not understand, chances

PREFACE

are that you will absorb more than you initially realize. As Lao tzu states in chapter 70, "My ideas are simple to grasp and easy to practice." Moreover, a preliminary reading of this sort will give you a sense concerning the dominant themes of the text as well as a feel for the way in which it is written.

After a holistic reading such as I have described in the preceding paragraph, you will be more prepared to focus your attention on specific chapters or themes. This time, do not simply nod a gesture of intellectual assent or shake your head with puzzlement. Pause to think about the content of the chapter. Reflect on your own life. Ask yourself: "Do I see the world in that way? Am I like that? What would it be like to approach life in that manner? Do I want to be like that?" Because these are not easy questions, do not expect the answers to come easily. Consider, for example, chapter 9:

> Sharpening excessively hastens up blunting.
> Filling to the brim leads to overflow.
> Stockpiling too much wealth invites thieves.
> Hankering after fame and fortune solicits catastrophe.
> After completing your work, rest.
> That is nature's way.

The first two lines make claims about what happens to physical objects when they are pushed beyond natural limitations. The next two contain a similar message regarding human desires for fame and fortune. The final two

PREFACE

provide practical advice that, without the context provided by the preceding lines, might seem rather trite or uninteresting. Given that context, however, the final lines take on profound significance in an easy-to-remember phrase. Because the phrase is so memorable, you can hold it in your mind long after you place the book back on the shelf. As you go through the day, you may find the passage returning again and again to your conscious awareness, challenging you to examine this or that particular activity in a new light. As you do, you may find that some things do not matter as much as you had previously believed. Over time you may find yourself doing less, worrying less, and enjoying life more. Such is the wisdom of the Tao Te Ching.

PREFACE

Introduction to Malhotra's Transcreation
Ronnie Littlejohn
Chair, Philosophy Department
Belmont University

The *Daodejing* (hereafter, DDJ) is the most translated into English of all the Chinese philosophical classics. It is divided into 81 "chapters" consisting of slightly over 5,000 Chinese characters, depending on which text is used. In its received form from Wang Bi the two major divisions of the text are the *dao jing* (chs. 1-37) and the *de jing* (chs. 38-81). Actually, this division probably rests on little else than the fact that the principal concept opening Chapter 1 is *dao* (way) and that of Chapter 38 is *de* (virtue).

The work is not just one more in a line of translations. The way in which Malhotra has grasped the meaning of an aphorism and recreated that meaning in English is the main value of this work. The transcreation is a result of a dialogue between Malhotra and the *Daodejing*. Malhotra understands the principal ideas of the *Daodejing* extraordinarily well. His long years of teaching Asian thought and his own practice and deep understanding of the meditative traditions of India, China and Japan gives him a unique insight into the text.

Malhotra's work is not only beautifully expressed but extremely clear. Consider his transcreation of the famous opening lines of Chapter One: 道可道; 非常道. 名可名; 非常名. While many translators get tangled up even in the opening lines, Malhotra is very clear: "Words that describe Tao, do not capture the real Tao; Names that

PREFACE

represent Tao, do not express the eternal Tao." Is this a so-called literal translation? No. But does it capture the meaning of the opening? Yes, emphatically so! There are many other places where the skill and grasp of the transcreator is evident. I commend to anyone evaluating this work Malhotra's transcreations of Chapter Ten, Twenty-nine, Thirty-five and many others. And yet, Malhotra does not ignore or go away from a strong connection to the text. Compare his translation of Chapter Forty-two with another recent transcreation (called a "philosophical translation") by Roger Ames and David Hall.

Hall and Ames (2003)	Malhotra (2006)
Way-making (*dao*) gives rise to continuity,	The Tao gave birth to one; one to two;
Continuity gives rise to difference,	two to three;
Difference gives rise to plurality,	and three produced the multiplicity of things.
And plurality gives rise to the manifold of everything that is happening (*wanwu*)	The multiplicity of things is embraced and balanced by the forces of female (Yin) and male (Yang).

So, while both of these recent works on the *Daodejing* are transcreations, Malhotra consistently shows a default back to the Wang Bi text. The connections of his version will always be recognizable by the reader who knows the Chinese text.

PREFACE

Malhotra knows the themes of the *Daodejing* very well. This grasp of the classic's teachings comes through in his chapter titles. Although the Chinese text has only number titles for the chapters, Malhotra tries to capture the theme of a chapter by giving it a title. Some scholars who feel that the composite nature of the *Daodejing* has been underappreciated in our work on this text will be somewhat uncomfortable with this approach because it might be taken to imply that each chapter is a unit and has a guiding theme. However, although the *Daodejing* is undoubtedly a cobbled together work, this does not mean that the work does not present a consistent vision or offer a repetition of coherent and expansive themes. As one scholar whose work is extremely dependent on the form and literary critical approach to the *Daodejing*, I can nevertheless say that I find Malhotra's chapter titles well conceived. I believe they will be extremely helpful even to the first time reader (perhaps especially to the first time reader). These titles reflect in many ways the most important themes of the classic: simplicity; forgetfulness; highest good is like water; overcome through yielding; merging with the Tao; the force within; by doing nothing, everything is done; the sage as a little child; and balance.

This work has much to commend it and its greatest strength is in the transcreator's own grasp of Daoism.

FOREWORD

One Saturday afternoon in July 1992, I was working on a manuscript, Pathways To Philosophy, when the telephone rang. As I reached for the phone, I was still engrossed in editing the manuscript. I said mechanically "good afternoon, this is Dr. Malhotra's office." The person on the other end said that it was Warner Brothers TV department. On hearing the name "Warner Brothers," I changed my intentional gear. To become attentive to the caller, I stopped typing the manuscript and asked the reason for the call. The caller was a women who introduced herself as a research assistant to Mr. Ken Parks, the lawyer for the Warner Brothers. I reiterated my original question, asking her the reason for the call. The conversation proceeded as follows:

Caller: "Warner Brothers is doing a new series called Kung Fu: The Legend Continues. The series will consist of 22 episodes, some of which will be shot in Toronto."
Ashok: "In what way can I help?"
Caller: "We are using some lines from an ancient manuscript from China or Japan. These lines will be spoken by David Carradine. We need your help in finding the source of these lines, as well as transforming these so that they could be used in the TV series."
Ashok: "How did you find my name and why do you think that I could help you with this project?"
Caller: "Our research department found your name

FOREWORD

                because you are a reputed scholar in this area."
Ashok: (in the state of half belief) "Could you please fax the text so that I could look at it? Here is my fax number."
Caller: "I am faxing you the text immediately. Please respond when you receive it. Thanks."
Ashok: "I am looking forward to receiving the text."

    After saying these words, I hung up the phone. I refused to believe my ears – that I had received a call from the Warner Brothers. I was convinced it was a joke on me by one of my disgruntled students. The fax arrived a few minutes later. I looked at the letterhead and it was from the research department of Warner Brothers. I could not believe my eyes! I glanced through the pages of the text and was surprised to see that they were from the Tao Te Ching of Lao Tzu. My surprise was due the fact that I had just finished a chapter on Taoism to be included in Pathways to Philosophy. I could not believe this miraculous coincidence.

    I readily accepted the offer from Warner Brothers. It was an exciting project because it required a creative transcreation of one of the most important Chinese philosophical texts. I was asked to transcreate lines from this ancient text in a language that could be easily understood by the general public, while keeping its literary excellence and philosophical profundity intact. To do so required bringing together the fields of philosophy,

FOREWORD

literature, and film.

After the TV Series was aired during the 1993-1994 season, I received many encouraging comments from scholars regarding my transcreation. Inspired by their remarks, I decided to transcreate the entire text of the *Tao Te Ching* for use by the undergraduate students as well as the general public. Since this book, which was written between 400 and 300 B.C.E., has been the third most translated work after the *Bible* and the *Bhagavad Gita*, and lives at many levels of meanings, my plan involves three distinct yet interrelated projects:

The First Project entails a unique transcreation of the entire text in a language that will be easily understood by a reader with or without any background in Chinese philosophy. Since I have studied the text carefully, attended a number of lectures and participated in a dozen conferences run by the International Society for Asian and Comparative Philosophy and the International Society for the Comparative Study of Civilizations, I have extensive notes on the *Tao Te Ching* which are being used for this transcreation. Furthermore, since I have used the *Tao Te Ching* in my undergraduate courses for 35 years, in the present transcreated text, the language and style are creatively used to appeal to the beginning students as well as to the general public.

The present work is the second project that involves the addition of art work into the text. Since the themes of

FOREWORD

the *Tao Te Ching* range from the beauty and spontaneity of nature to the human foibles of aggressiveness and wars and to the gift of a simple contented life, the transcreated text is being embellished through the introduction of art work and photographs. These works of art are my original paintings, which capture through lines, colors, and harmonious forms, the essence of the philosophical message. Besides the paintings, a number of photographs of various natural scenes are also incorporated into the book. The translated text is on one page whereas the paintings and photographs, which capture the experiential aspect of each theme, are on the adjacent page. There are eighty-one pages of translated text, as well as eighty-one paintings and photographs depicting important themes.

The Third Project involves creating a CD-ROM of the artistically transcreated text of the *Tao Te Ching*.

A number of people who have generously contributed to the completion of the first phase of the project deserve my heartfelt thanks. Of special mention is Professor Chung-ying Cheng who introduced me to Chinese philosophy when I was a grantee at the East West Center and a student at the University of Hawaii. Furthermore, I have benefitted a great deal from reading the works of Wing-tsit Chan, Herbert Fingarette, Henry Rosemont, John Koller, Philip Ivanhoe, Roger Ames and David Hall. They have guided me through this arduous and challenging journey of making sense of Chinese philosophy, as well as this difficult yet profound text. Since I made use of at least a dozen major translations

FOREWORD

of the *Tao Te Ching*, I am indebted to these scholars. At a professional level, thanks are due to Professors Roger Ames of the University of Hawaii and Ronnie Littlejohn of Belmont University for reading the entire manuscript and offering their insightful comments. Special thanks go to Dr. Douglas Shrader, SUNY Distinguished Teaching Professor and Chairman of the Philosophy Department at SUNY Oneonta, for reading the entire manuscript and offering crucial amendments. Finally, it is Marge Holling who ends up doing all the hard work to make the manuscript ready for publication. I will never be able to thank her enough. The present work is the second phase of the project where photographs in the book as well as on front and back covers appear courtesy of Ms. Linda Drake. Thanks are due to Ian Lascell for improving the design of the book cover and to Diana Moseman for converting the entire manuscript to the PDF format as well as adding paintings and photographs to the entire text.

Ashok Kumar Malhotra
June 2, 2013

Introduction
to the Tao Te Ching

There has been a great deal of controversy about the life of Lao Tzu and the text of the Tao Te Ching.

Stories about Lao Tzu's life range from legends to mythology.

One of the legends depicts Lao Tzu as an older contemporary of Confucius who challenged some of the basic principles of Confucian philosophy.

Another regards Lao Tzu as an old master who was endowed with such extraordinary wisdom that he had grey hair at birth.

A third one characterizes him as the keeper of the royal archives, who lived during the troubled times when the inter-state rivalry kept the selfish rulers warring with each other for a few hundred years.

Another one portrays Lao Tzu as a sensitive and caring human being who regarded wars as evil; rulers as power hungry beasts; government as bastian of corruption; and supporters of the ruler and government as greedy, selfish and ambitious human beings, who fought and killed each other for personal gain and aggrandizement.

Another popular legend points out that Lao Tzu was so repulsed by wars, the rulers, selfishness of the people and

INTRODUCTION

the breakdown of law and order, that he left his country and headed south. When he reached the southernmost part of his land and as he tried to enter the new country, the guard stopped him. On questioning by the guard, Lao Tzu indicated his disenchantment and discontent with his country of birth and his reasons for abandoning it. The guard who listened to Lao Tzu's tale with great interest asked him to jot down his insightful thoughts before he could be given permission to enter this new country. The legend dramatizes Lao Tzu as stringing together his pearls of wisdom carefully in a short book which came to be called the *Tao Te Ching* or "The Way and Its Power."

The text of the *Tao Te Ching* has its own history of controversy in terms of the date, the content and the authorship. The most recent consensus puts the text between 400 and 300 B.C.E. Since the traditional text is partly poetic and partly prose and indicates various styles of writing, it might have been written by different scholars besides Lao Tzu. The traditional compiled text of the *Tao Te Ching* was first commented upon by Wang Bi in 249 C.E.

This version of the text has been the focal point of most of the latter commentaries. Wang Bi divided the text into two parts. The first 37 chapters, which constitute Book One, present the nature of the Tao whereas the last 44 chapters, which make up Book Two, reveal the nature of the Te. Since this classification of the *Tao Te Ching* text covering 81 chapter into two books has been the model for the commentators for almost two thousand years, we will

INTRODUCTION

follow this arrangement in the ordering of our present translation.

THE TRANSCREATED TEXT

OF THE

TAO TE CHING

WITH PHOTOGRAPHS

BOOK ONE
(Chapters 1-37)

Ashok Kumar Malhotra

Chapter 1

The Tao

Words that describe Tao, do not capture the real Tao;
Names that represent Tao, do not express the eternal Tao.
The nameless is the source of heaven and earth;
The named is the source of all particular things.
Through desirelessness, the unnamed is experienced as oneness;
Through desire, the named is experienced as manifested things.
The nameless and the named are alike because they originate from the same source;
They are diverse because they are described differently;
Their ineffable source is a deep cosmic mystery;
One who comprehends this profound connection between the nameless and the named attains total wisdom.

Wisdom of the Tao Te Ching

Chapter 2

Contraries

When something is called as beautiful,
something else becomes ugly;
When something is named as good,
something else becomes evil.
Existence and non–existence cause each other;
Happiness and unhappiness depend upon each other;
Long and short are understood through each other;
High and low rest upon each other;
Before and after follow each other.
A sage grasps these contraries and
Acts without action;
Teaches without words;
Witnesses the ebb and flow of events;
Creates without appropriation;
Achieves without claiming;
When the work is done,
the sage forgets it and
the achievement lasts for ever.

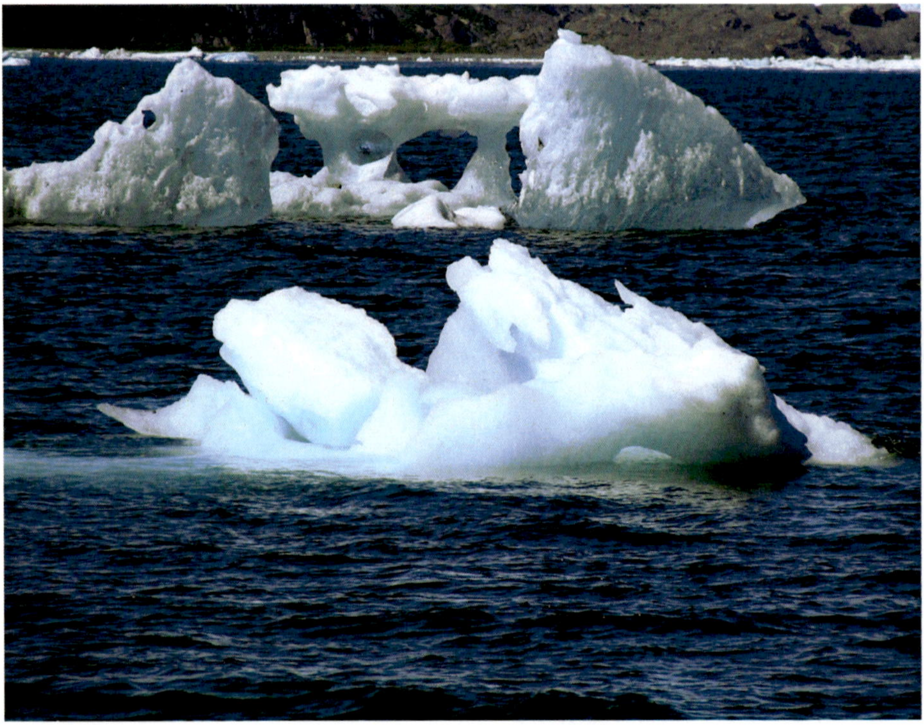

Ashok Kumar Malhotra

Chapter 3

Going with the Flow

When the learned are glorified;
rivalry is amplified.
When possessions are treasured;
stealing becomes rampant.
When desires are perpetuated;
people's emotions run wild.
Therefore, a sage governs:
by emptying people's hearts,
by filling their bellies,
by lessening their ambition,
by strengthening their bodily frame,
by freeing them from knowing and desiring,
and by not letting the shrewd ones pollute the innocent minds.
By acting in accordance with the natural flow of events,
a sage practices non–action.

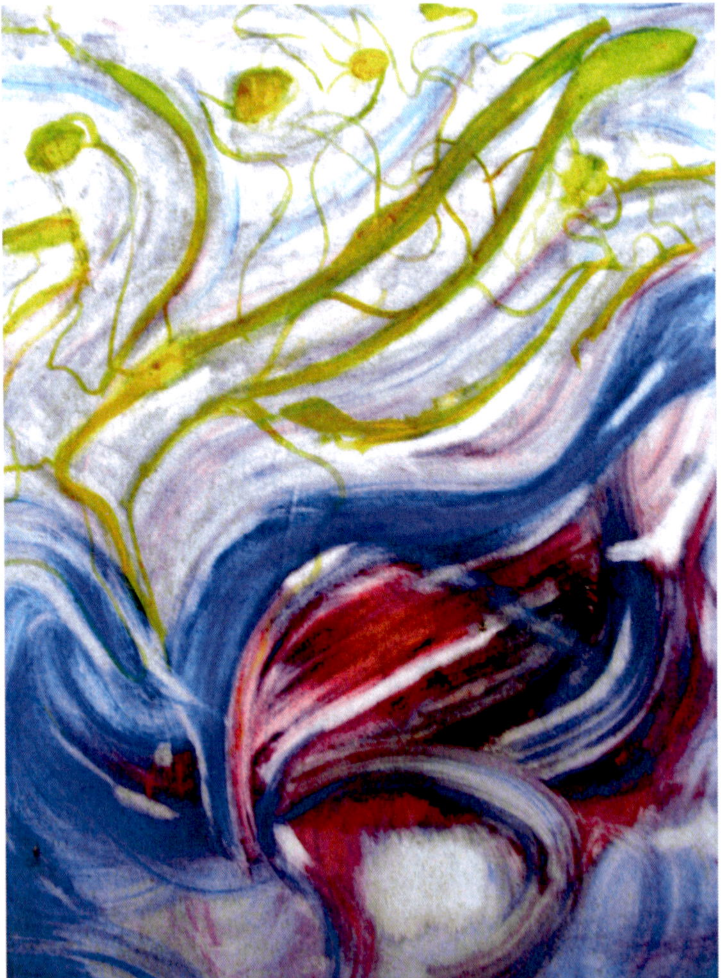

Wisdom of the Tao Te Ching

Chapter 4

The Mysterious Tao

Tao is formless
and yet it fills everything.
Tao is bottomless,
and yet it is the source of everything.
Tao smoothens rough edges,
undoes knots,
controls all glare,
is one with the dust,
is all pervasive,
and yet it is ever hidden.
Who knows where it sprang from?
It is more ancient than the most ancient.

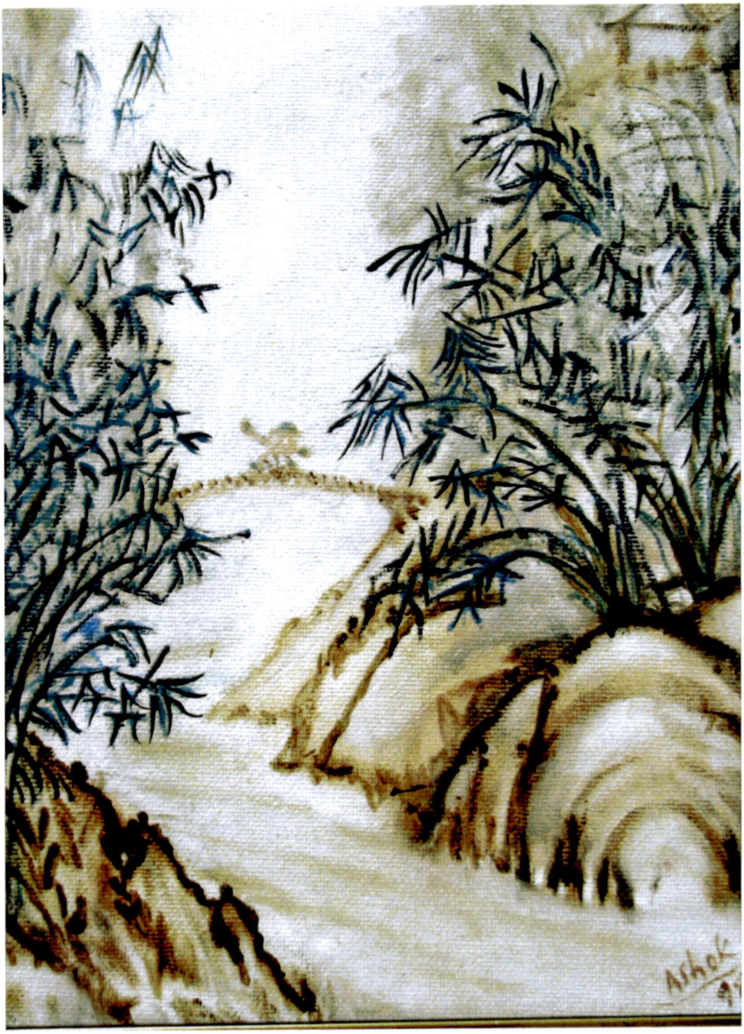
Ashok

Ashok Kumar Malhotra

Chapter 5

Tao and Sage

Tao is aloof
because it is unattached to the created things.
The sage is aloof
because he is unattached to human beings.
Like a bellows is the universe,
inexhaustibly empty,
and yet continuously creating.
Words are unable to capture it
and yet it is available
to one who is centered.

-14-

Chapter 6

The Great Mother

Tao is the mystic mother
who is all pervasive.
She gives birth to everything,
resides within everyone,
and is readily available.

-16-

Ashok Kumar Malhotra

Chapter 7

Compassion for Others

Tao lasts forever.
Why?
Because it is uncreated.
Tao is enduring
Why?
Because it is there for others.
The sage is ahead.
Why?
Because she is always behind.
The sage is present everywhere.
Why?
Because she is unattached.
The sage is fulfilled.
Why?
Because she does not seek anything.

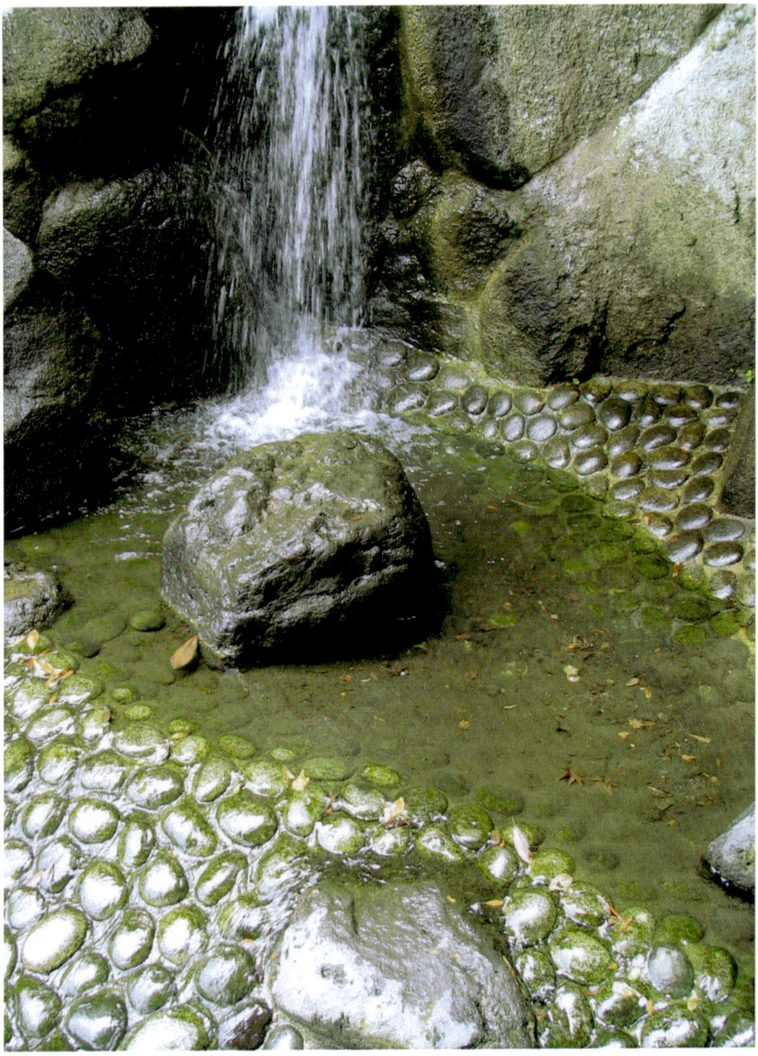

Wisdom of the Tao Te Ching

Chapter 8

Highest Good is Like Water

The highest good is like water.
It nurtures everything without effort.
It flows in the most lowly places without repugnance.
Similar to the Tao,
it dwells
in the humble earth;
in the simple thinking;
in the truthful speech;
in the fair treatment of others;
in the work competently done;
and in the family affairs.
The good person does not compete
and thus is respected by everyone.

-20-

Ashok Kumar Malhotra

Chapter 9

Step Back

Sharpening excessively hastens up blunting.
Filling to the brim leads to overflow.
Stockpiling too much wealth invites thieves.
Hankering after fame and fortune solicits catastrophe.
After completing your work, rest.
That is nature's way.

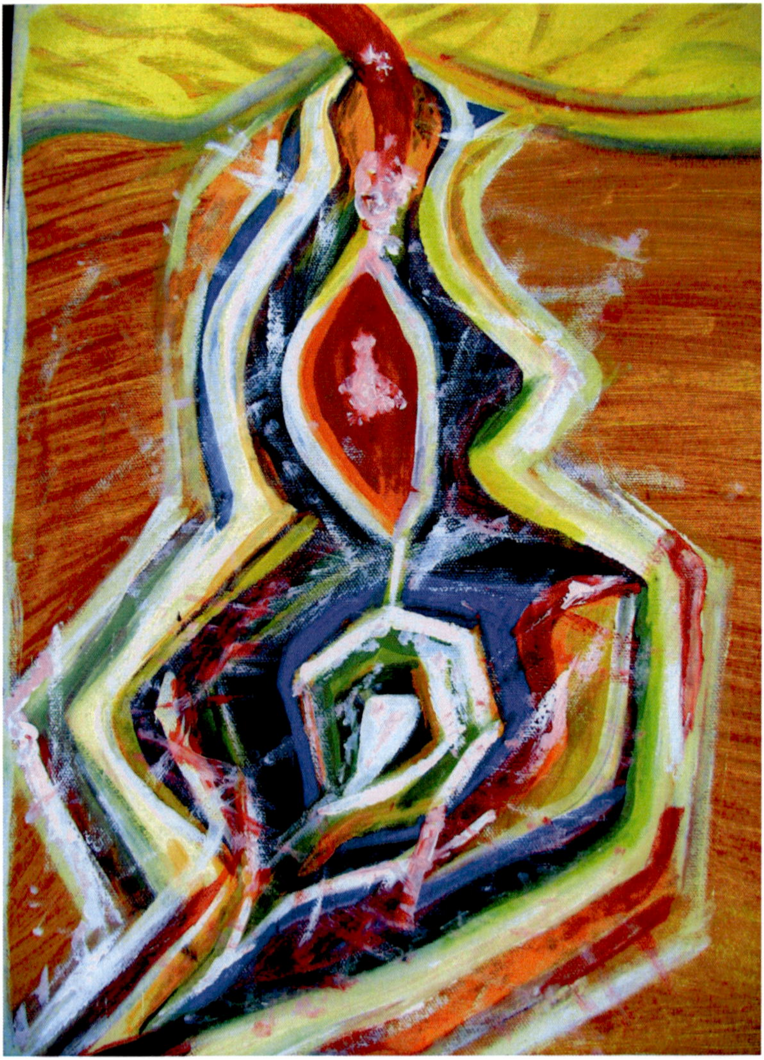

Wisdom of the Tao Te Ching

Chapter 10

Nature of the Inner Power

Can you arrest your mind from the restless wanderings and still focus on the Tao?
Can you control your vital force like an infant?
Can you purify your inner vision without staining?
Can you guide without ordering?
Can you indulge in significant events in accordance with their natural flow?
Can you gain knowledge without the help of the mind?
Always creating, nourishing, non-possessing, acting without reward, and leading without controlling is the way of the inner power (Te).

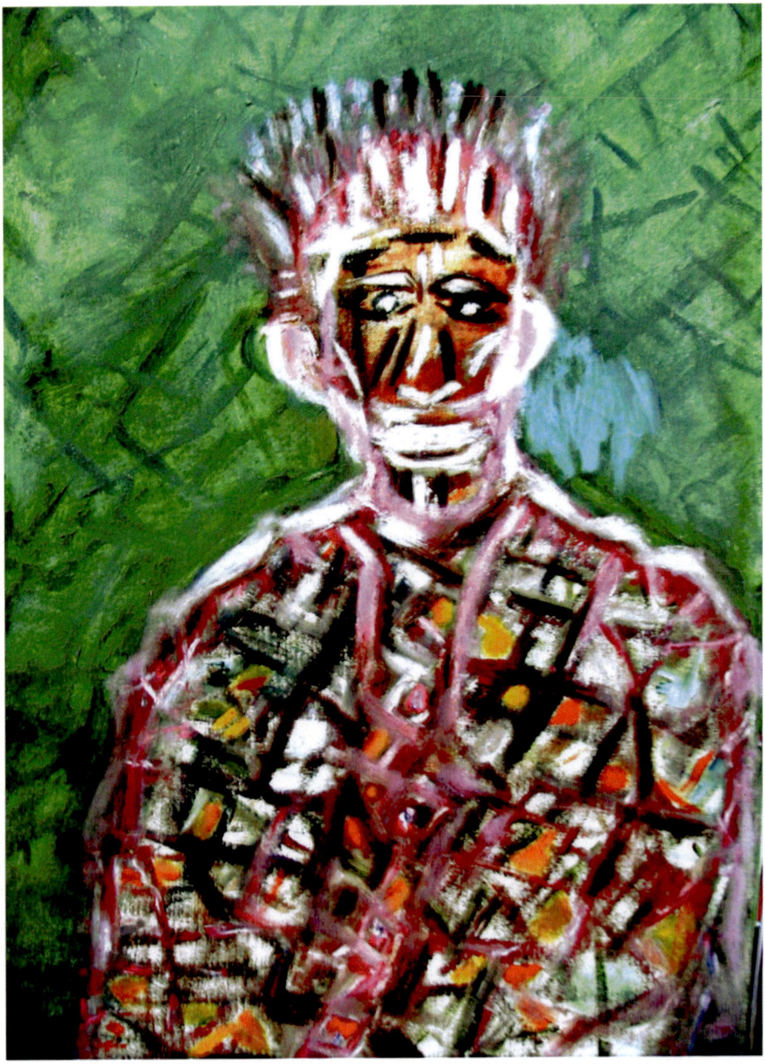

Ashok Kumar Malhotra

Chapter 11

Usefulness of Emptiness

Many spokes make up the wheel,
but the emptiness of the central hole makes it workable.
A pot is formed from the clay,
but the empty space within makes it usable.
Doors and windows form the walls of a house,
but their openness makes them useful.
A person profits from the existence of things,
but is nourished by their non-existence.

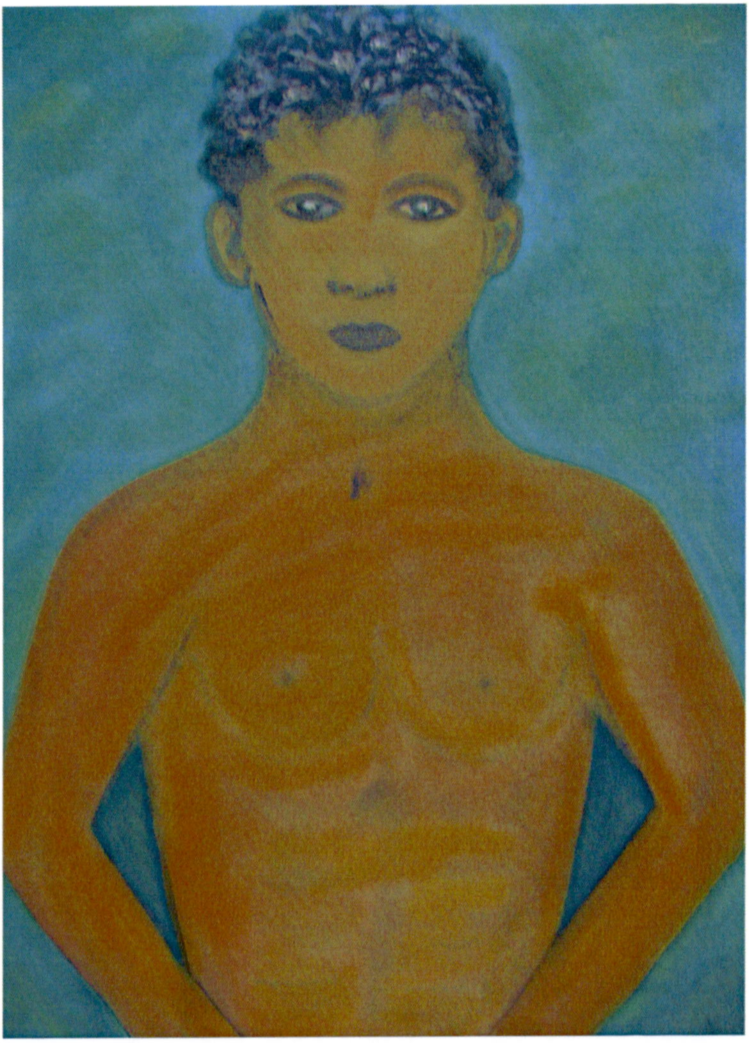

Wisdom of the Tao Te Ching

Chapter 12

Senses versus Inner Vision

An ordinary person's
eyes are blinded by colors;
ears are deafened by sounds;
tastes are clogged by flavors;
and mind is distracted by desires.
However, a sage experiences
the world through senses
and yet relies upon the inner vision;
says no to one and yes to the other.

-28-

Chapter 13

Oppositions

Favor and disfavor are equally burdensome;
Success and failure are equally painful.
How can favor and disfavor be equally troublesome?
By receiving a favor, one is degraded;
By not receiving a favor one is also belittled.
How can success and failure be equally painful?
Whether you go up or down, both stages are shaky;
Treat the world as yourself, it will become your abode;
Love the world as yourself, it will become your own.

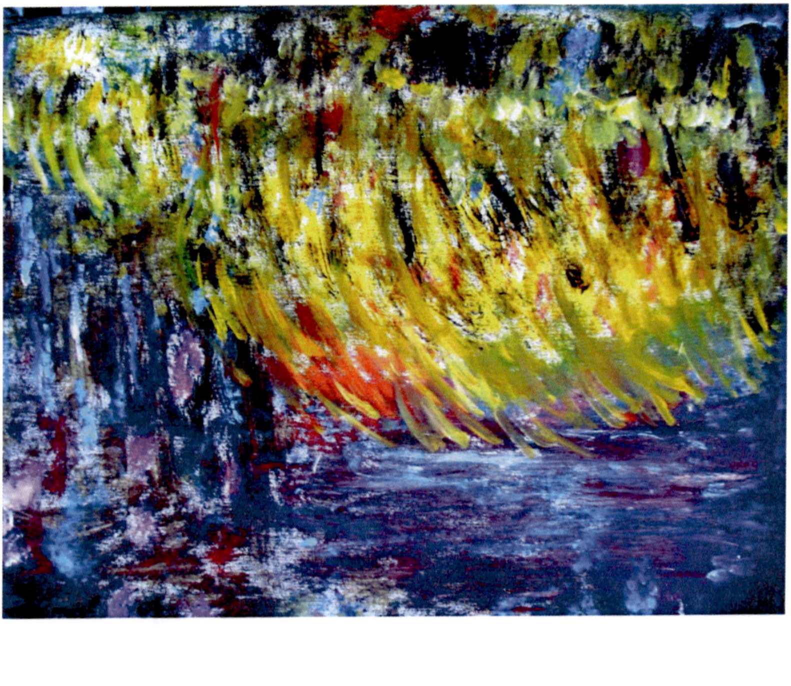

Wisdom of the Tao Te Ching

Chapter 14

The Ineffable Tao

When you try to look, it can not be seen;
When you try to listen, it can not be heard;
When you try to appropriate, it can not be grasped.
These three constitute the ineffable character of the one.
It is not the brightness above.
It is not the darkness below.
It is all encompassing.
It defies all definitions.
It is no-thing.
As the formless form of all forms,
and the imageless image of all images,
it excludes all conception and imagination.
When you face it, you find it without a beginning.
When you follow it, you find it endless.
When you are fully engrossed in the ancient Tao,
while living in the now,
you will experience the secret of wisdom.

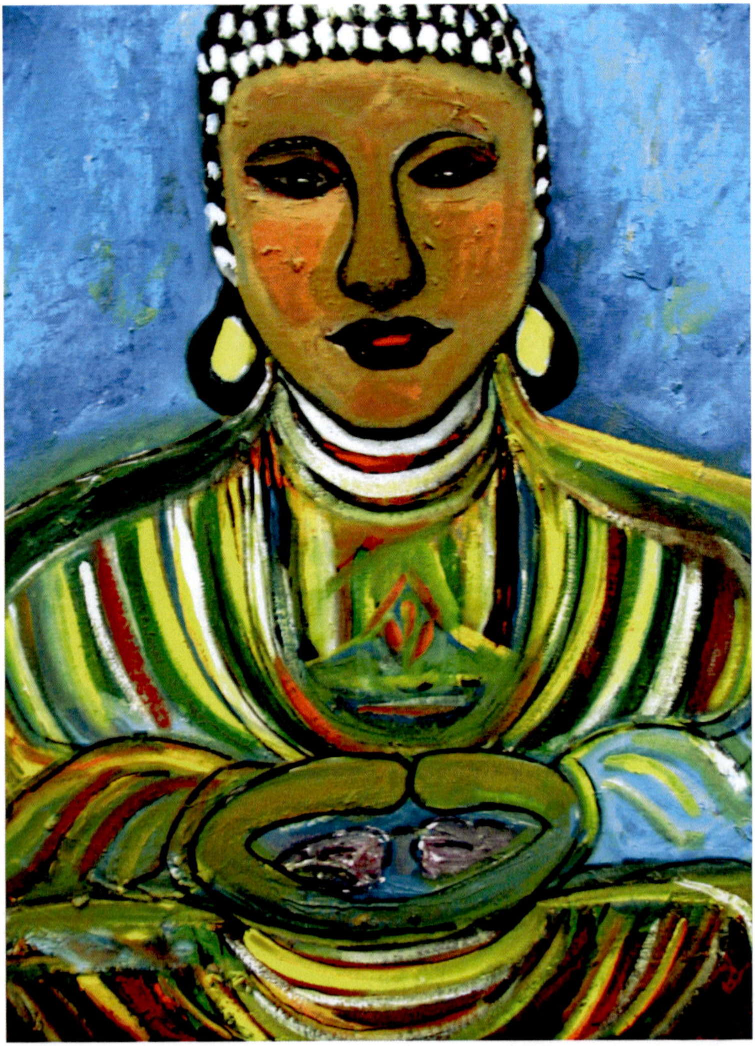

Ashok Kumar Malhotra

Chapter 15

Wise Sages

The sages of the ancient were profound,
because they possessed subtle wisdom and deep understanding.
Their prodigious knowledge could be grasped only superficially,
because they could be described only metaphorically as:
Wakeful: like passing an icy creek.
Vigilant: like a fugitive.
Thoughtful: Like a guest.
Yielding: Like melting ice.
Pliable: like a block of wood.
Alluring: like a valley.
Freely mixing: like muddy water.
Resting: like settling of muddy water to clearness.
Remaining still: till the opportune moment arises for action.
Because the sages own nothing and seek no-thing, all gifts come to them.

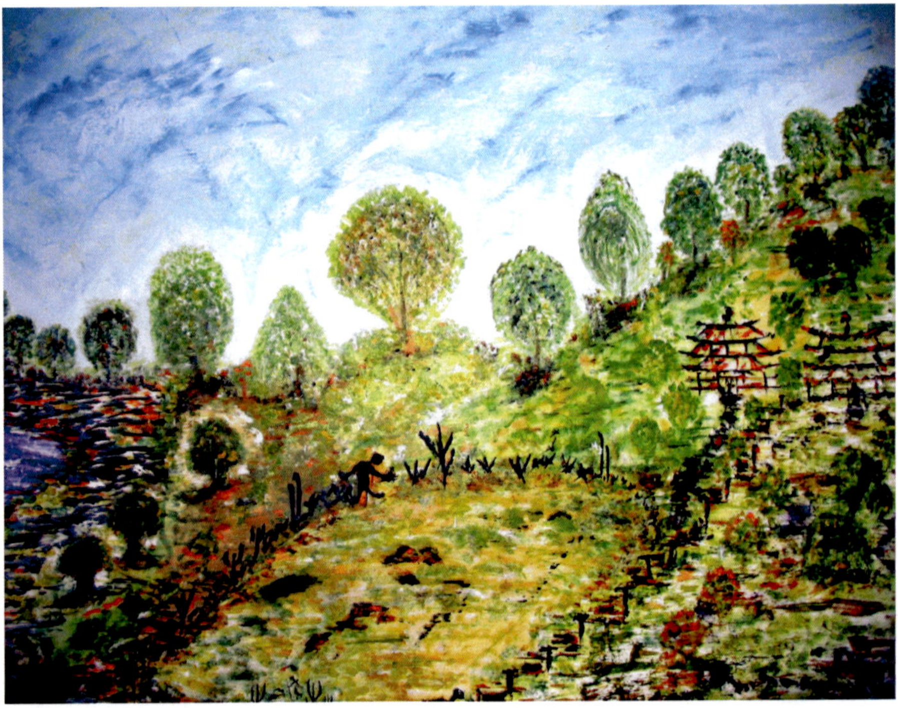

Wisdom of the Tao Te Ching

Chapter 16

The Source

Make your mind blank;
Still your heart;
Watch the frenzy of people;
Look attentively to how people return to their source;
Eventually all people go back to their source.
Homecoming to the source brings repose;
If you are confused about the source;
you are doomed.
But if you are in touch with the source;
you become broad minded,
equitable, regal, and kindhearted.
Because you are going with the universal flow of the Tao,
you can meet with any challenge of life.
This is a wonderful preparation
for the final merging into the restful abode of the Tao.

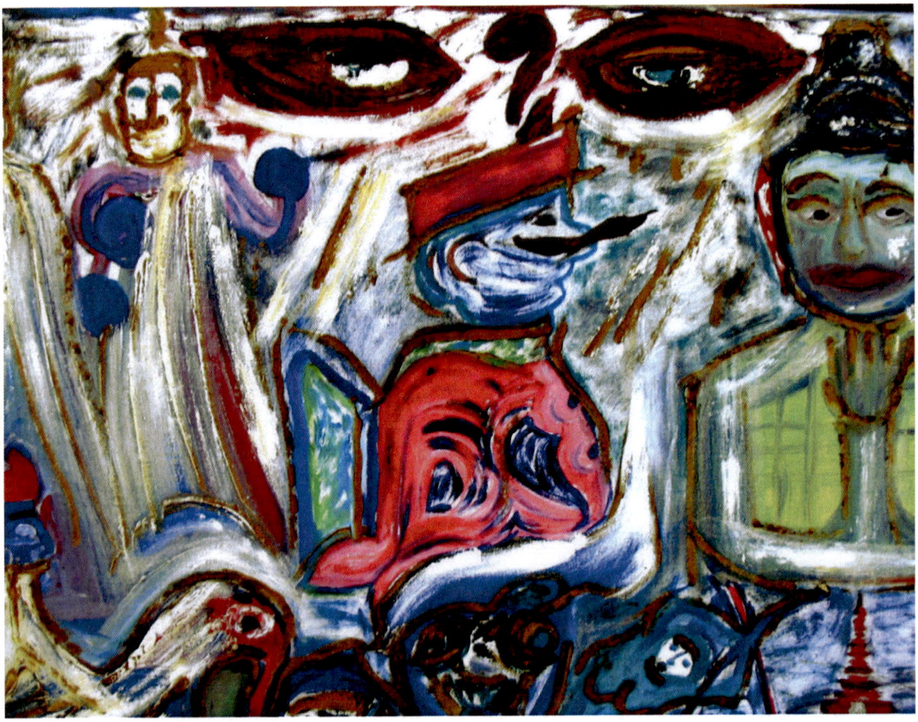

Ashok Kumar Malhotra

Chapter 17

Who is the Best Leader?

The best leader is one who is least obvious,
the second best is one that people think they know and love,
the third one is that to whom people fear,
and next one is that to whom people despise.
A leader who does not respect people does not fetch their respect.
Thus, the best leader acts without dictating.
When her work is done;
people think they did it all by themselves.

-38-

Chapter 18

Forgetfulness of the Tao

When one becomes oblivious to the great Tao,
morality and conventions are born.
When knowledge and shrewdness take roots,
hypocrisy spreads.
When dissension in the family relationships arise,
filial pity results.
And when the country starts breaking apart at its seams,
patriotism becomes the vogue.

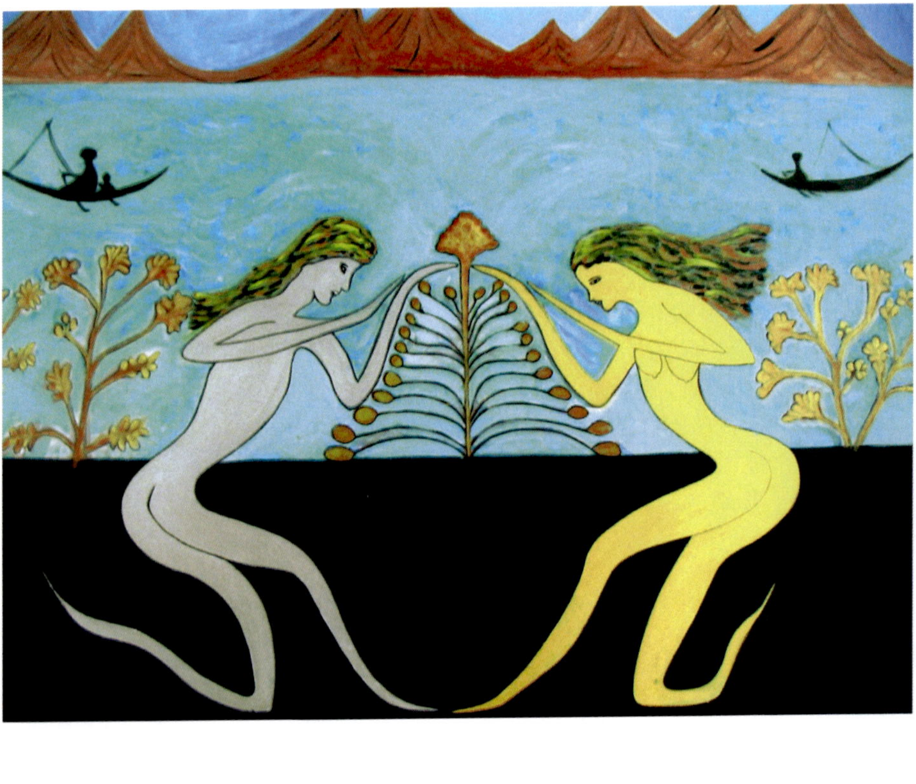

Chapter 19

Simplicity

Empty yourself of knowledge and wisdom,
you will gain pure happiness.
Become oblivious to morality and conventions,
you will find the natural correct path.
Get away from cunning and profiteering,
thievery will also disappear.
Abandon these three,
you will realize the simplicity
of your true nature devoid of selfishness and desire.

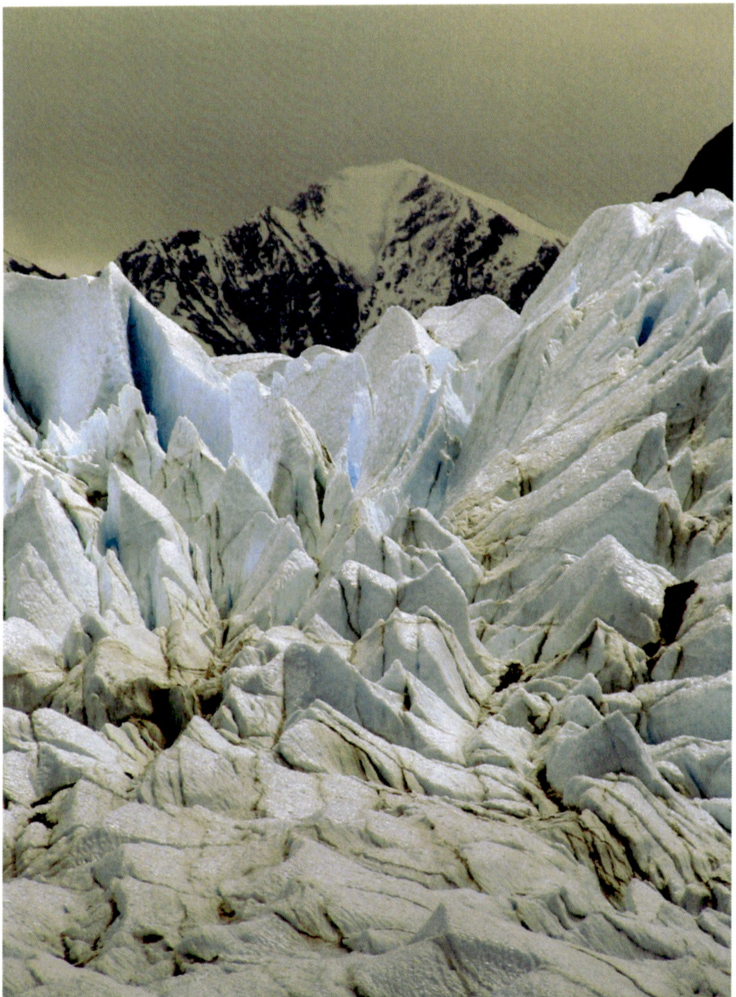

Wisdom of the Tao Te Ching

Chapter 20

Nourished by the Great Mother

By stilling the analytic mind and you will gain peace.
What difference is there between yes and no?
What difference is there between good and bad?
Why do what everybody else does?
What others do might appear to be attractive?
Because they are feasting,
basking in the Spring, and
climbing the mountain.
But I am alone without a set path;
like a new-born child who has not yet learned to smile.
While others have too much,
I own nothing;
I am a simpleton who is innocent.
While others are bright and cheery,
I am unpolished and depressed.
While others are cunning and crisp,
I am dull and sloppy.
I am a drifter like the waves of the ocean,
and aimless wanderer like the wind.
While others have purpose, I am without a goal.
Totally unlike others,
I am nourished by the Great Mother.

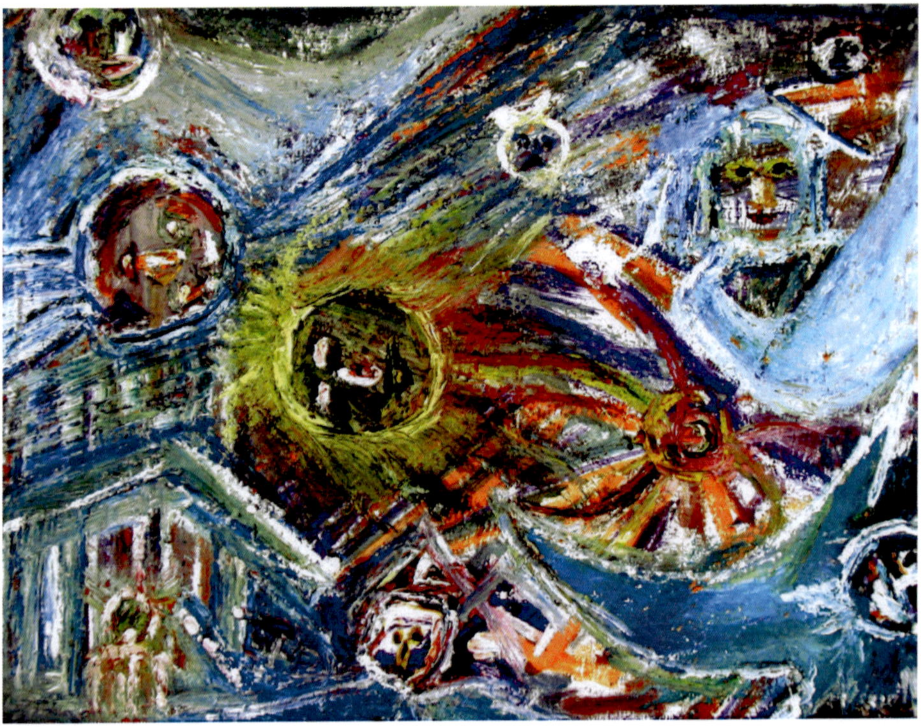

Ashok Kumar Malhotra

Chapter 21

Mark of the Tao

Te is the mark of Tao in everything.
Though Tao is ineffable,
all forms are potentially within it.
Though Tao is elusive,
all objects are dormant in it.
Though Tao is impenetrable and indefinite,
all life-force lies hidden in it.
And though Tao is the farthest away,
it is at the core of every manifest being.
How do we grasp the mother of everything?
Through its stamp on each created thing.

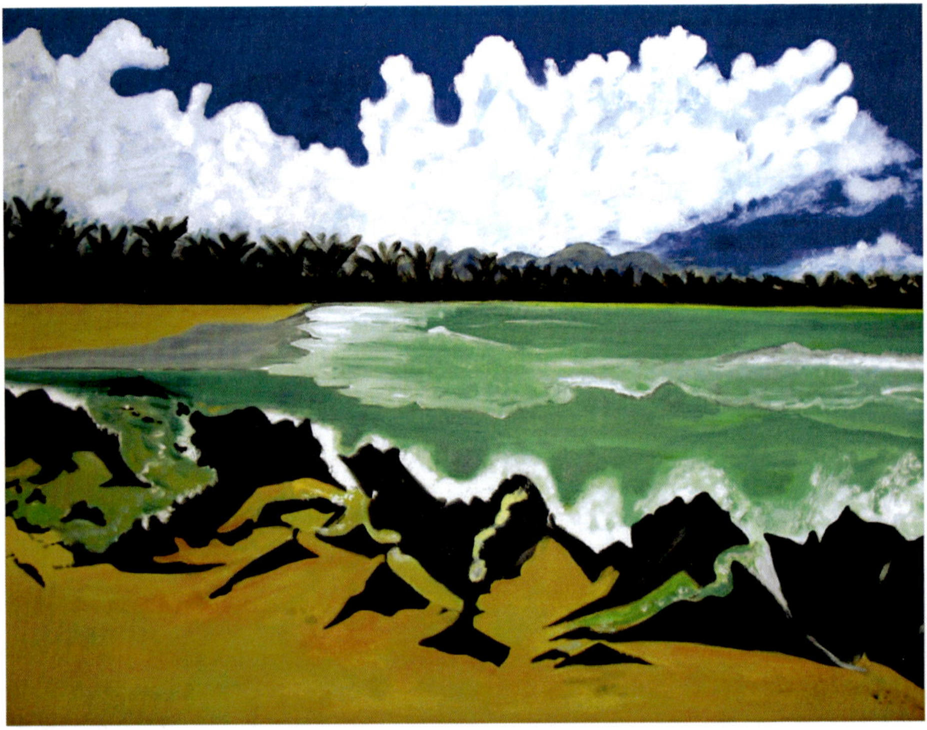

Chapter 22

Overcome Through Yielding

By yielding one overcomes;
By bending one becomes straight;
By emptying one becomes full;
By fraying, one is renewed;
By giving away one possesses;
And by having too much one is disoriented.
So by embracing the Tao,
the sage sets up an example for the others.
By not standing out,
she shines forth.
By not having anything to prove,
she earns distinction.
By being humble,
she gets fame.
By not bragging,
people take pride in her.
And by not being antagonistic toward others,
others are not antagonistic toward her.
The truth of the ancient maxim "overcome through yielding" is attested by the wise sage who by giving everything up gains everything back.

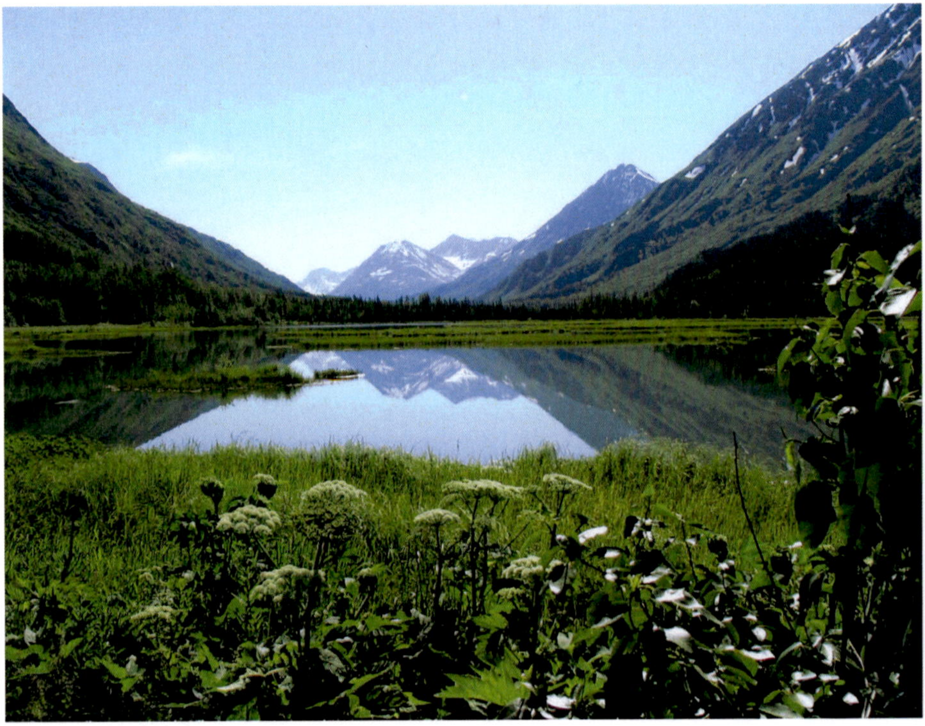

Chapter 23

Merging into the Tao

Tao speaks very little!
Turbulent winds do not last all morning!
Rain storms do not continue all day!
Where do they originate?
From the manifest Tao!
If the manifest Tao speaks so little,
why should not the human being?
One who follows the way (Tao),
merges into it.
One who follows one's inner nature (Te),
expresses it.
One who is estranged from the way,
experiences one's alienation from it.
When one identifies with Tao,
one is accepted by it.
When one identifies with one's nature (Te),
one is greeted by it.
And one who abandons it,
experiences the abdication.
Thus one who trusts the way (Tao),
merges into it.

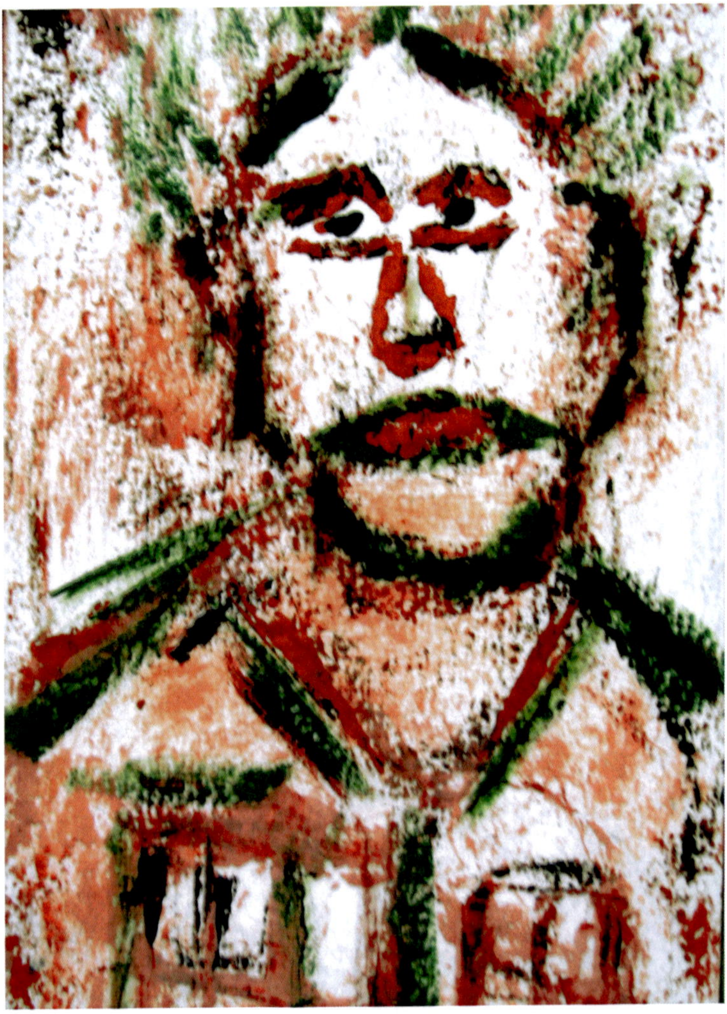

Wisdom of the Tao Te Ching

Chapter 24

What the Sage Avoids?

By standing on tiptoes, one loses balance.
By rushing, one makes no advance.
By showing off, one dims one's light.
By advertising oneself, one recedes from fame.
By boasting about one's virtues, one earns discredit.
By showing pride, one is far from becoming a leader.
According to the adherents of the way (Tao), this extra baggage leads to no happiness.
Thus the sage avoids it at all costs.

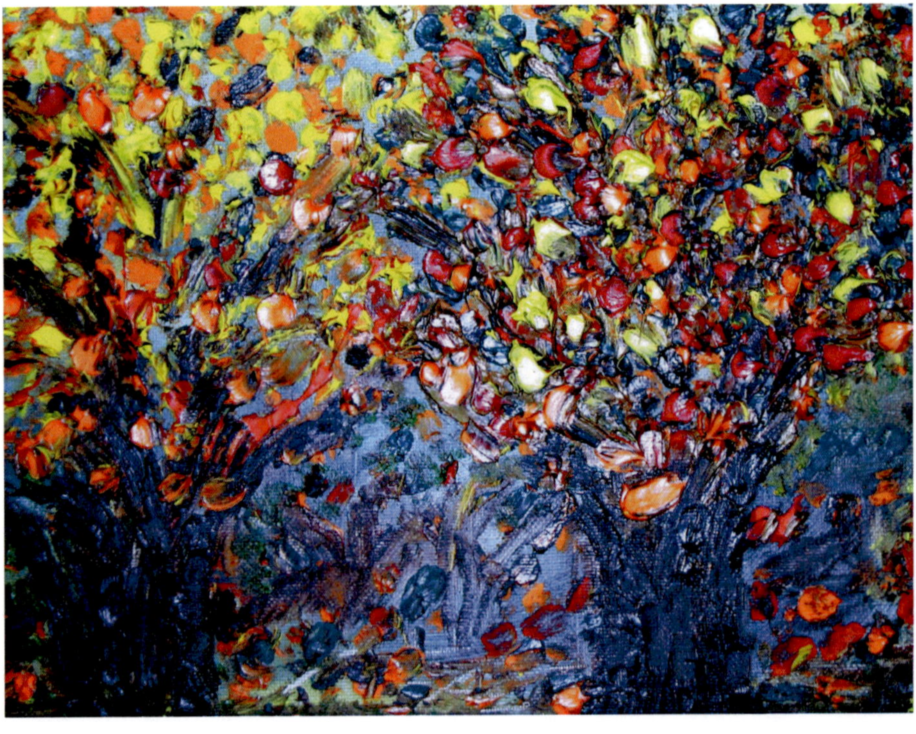

Ashok Kumar Malhotra

Chapter 25

Nature of the Tao

Before the universe came to be,
there existed the silent, solitary, unchanging,
undifferentiated, ineffable being.
Because this all-encompassing source of everything is nameless,
it may be called the Tao or better still the "Great One."
Tao is great because it is all "enveloping" and encloses everything within itself.
There are four greats:
the Tao,
the universe,
the earth,
and the human being.
The human being follows the earth,
the earth follows the universe,
the universe follows the Tao
and the Tao follows itself.

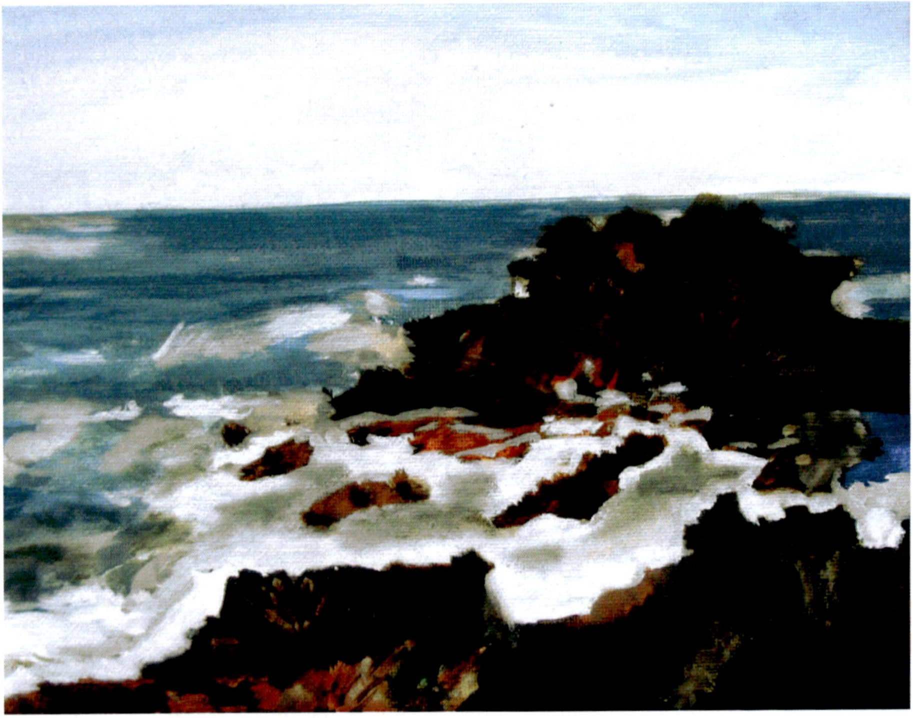

Wisdom of the Tao Te Ching

Chapter 26

Contrasts

Enduring stability is the root of the frivolous lightness of freedom;
Stillness is the source of all movement.
Thus the sage journeys all day while staying at home.
Despite the wondrous distractions, the sage remains calm and collected.
How can the great ruler make light of these distractions?
She knows that to be free leads to disconnection with the enduring stability and to be restless means losing control of oneself.

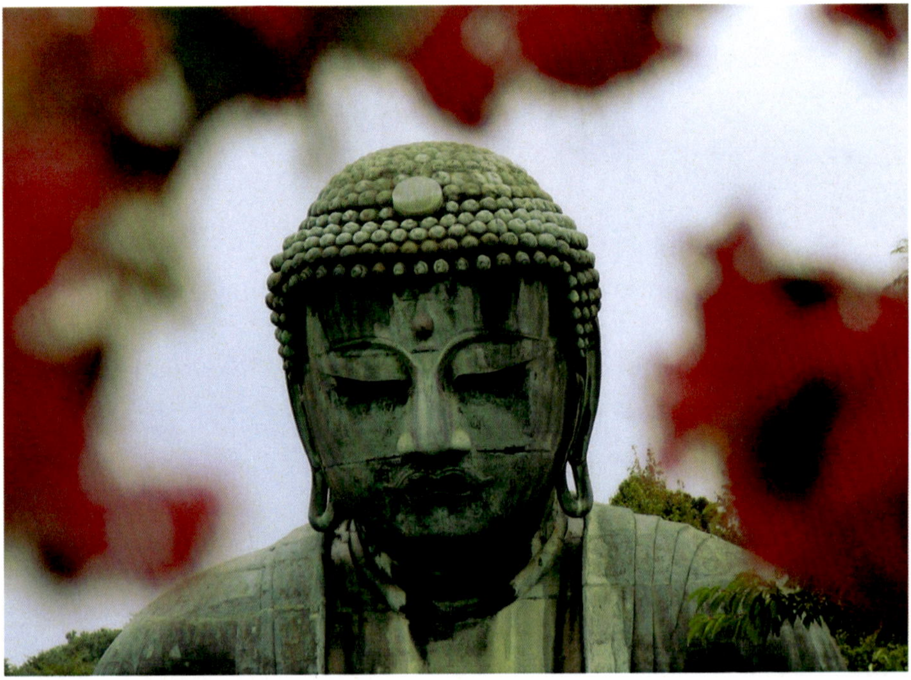

Ashok Kumar Malhotra

Chapter 27

Wondrous Secret

A skillful traveler leaves no traces.
A good speaker speaks without any flaws.
An excellent reckoner needs no aids.
An expert door hanger requires no bolts.
And a good binder needs no threads.
Thus, a sage helps all people without discrimination
and resolves problems without turning away from them.
This ability of the sage is called "insightful wisdom."
The sage is the teacher of the un-sage-like person and the
un-sage-like person is the subject-matter for the sage.
One who does not respect one's teacher or the teaching,
though is learned, has gone astray.
This is a "wondrous secret."

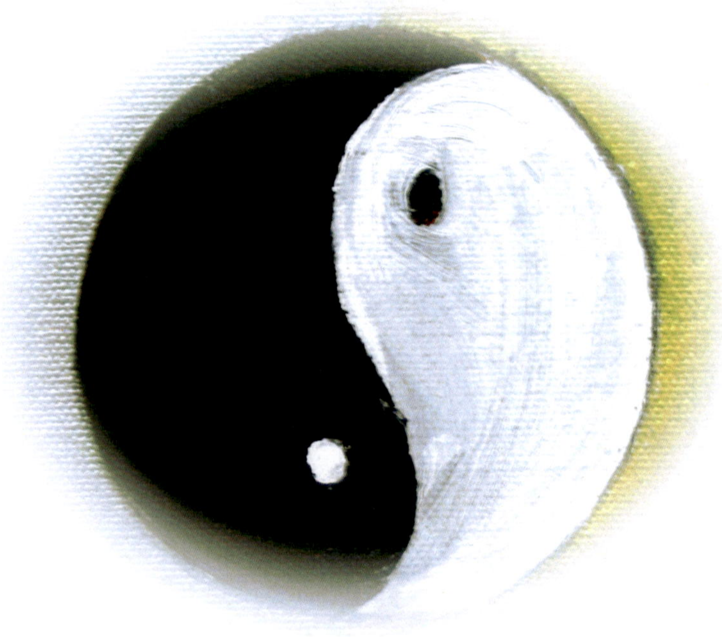

Wisdom of the Tao Te Ching

Chapter 28

The Force Within (Te)

When you know the male
and keep to the female,
you hold the universe in your hands.
When you hold the universe in your hands,
the inner force (Te) will always be with you
and you will become like an innocent child.
When you are aware of the light
and keep it to the darkness,
you will become a model for the universe to imbibe.
When you are an example for the universe,
your inner force will manifest in every one of your actions
and you will be capable of doing anything.
When you know name and fame
but keep yourself closer to obscurity,
you will be in touch with the inner force.
When you apprehend the inner force,
you will feel the Tao
and experience the connection with the uncarved block of reality.
From this uncarved block,
the diversity of things is created.
Since the sage grasps the connection between the
uncarved block and the carved universe,
she stays close to the pristine simplicity (Tao).

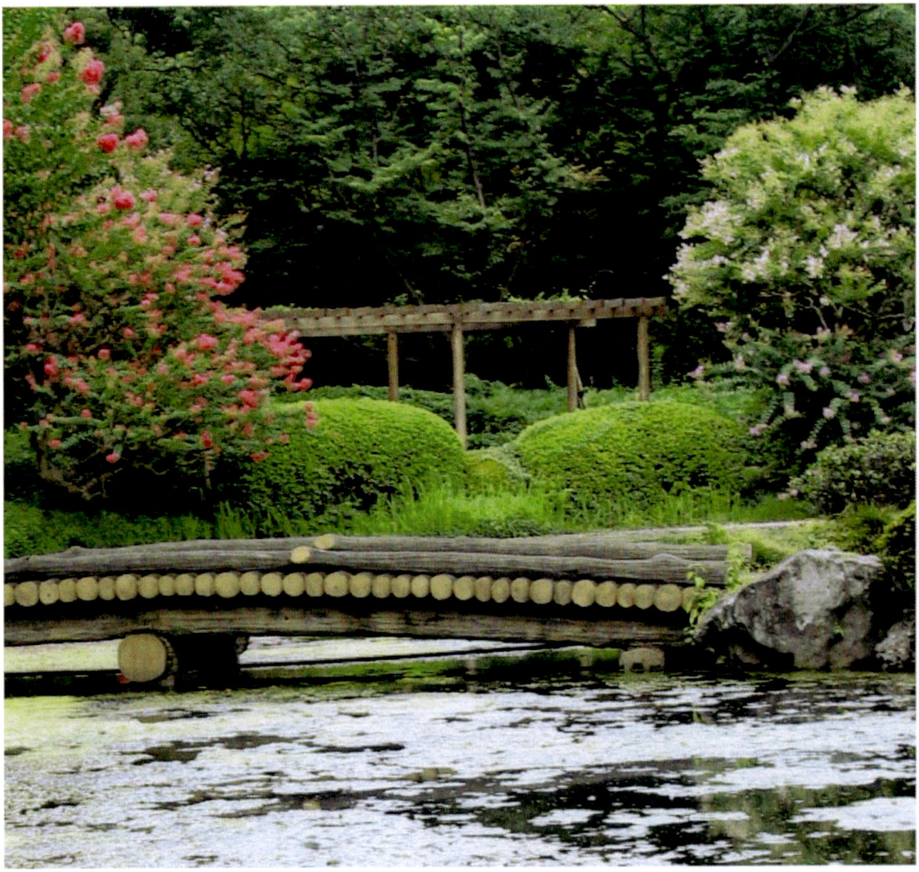

Ashok Kumar Malhotra

Chapter 29

Avoiding Extremes

Those who want to mold the universe to perfect it
will find that it cannot be done.
The universe is a sacred vessel,
which cannot be controlled.
When you try to modify it,
you destroy it
and when you try to possess it,
you lose it.
The universe offers the opportunity
to go ahead or stay behind;
to make noise or be silent;
to become strong or to stay weak;
to oppress or be oppressed.
Thus, the sage avoids extremes, extravagance and arrogance.

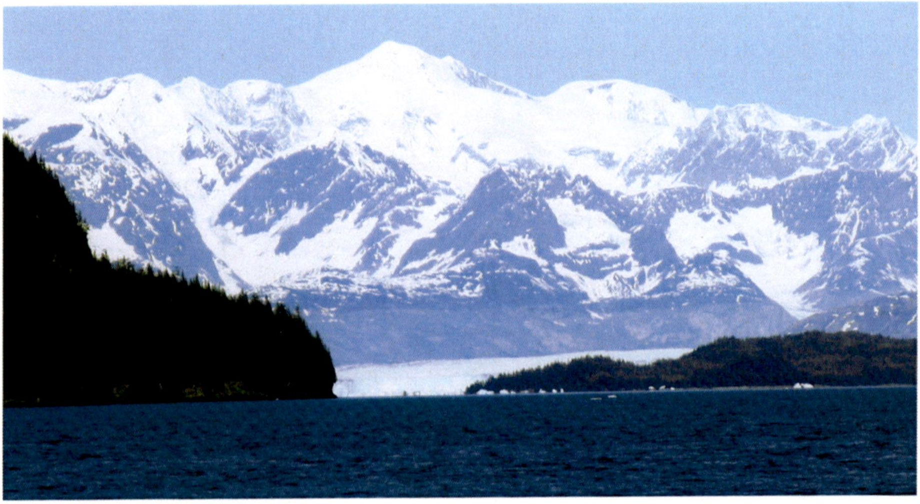

Wisdom of the Tao Te Ching

Chapter 30

Use of Force

To rule according to the way of the Tao decries the use of force;
because the use of force is counter-productive to achieving the ends.
Just like thorns and bushes sprout up after the army has passed over them;
great wars lead to great devastations.
A sage never misuses force.
She acts and achieves results,
without hankering after glory.
She acts and achieves results without boasting.
She acts and achieves results without being overbearing.
She acts and achieves results without being arrogant.
She acts and achieves results in a natural way without being violent.
Thus, when one does not lead a life in conformity with Tao, one comes to an early end.

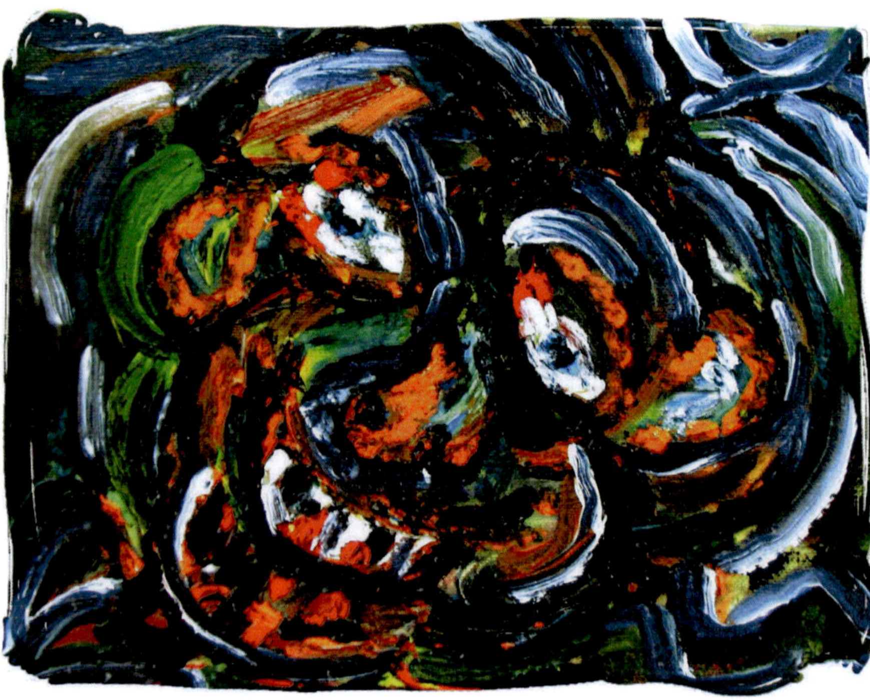

Ashok Kumar Malhotra

Chapter 31

Evil of Weapons

Weapons of war are hated by everyone including the followers of Tao.
Weapons of war are tools of terror, which are not the devices of the sage.
The sage will utilize them cautiously and only as a last resort because he believes in the calm restraint.
The weapons of war are not beautiful.
Those who think they are beautiful,
rejoice in mass slaughter.
And those who take delight in mass carnage,
will not be successful in controlling the world.
The sage takes part in a war with great sadness and sorrow as if he were joining a funeral procession.

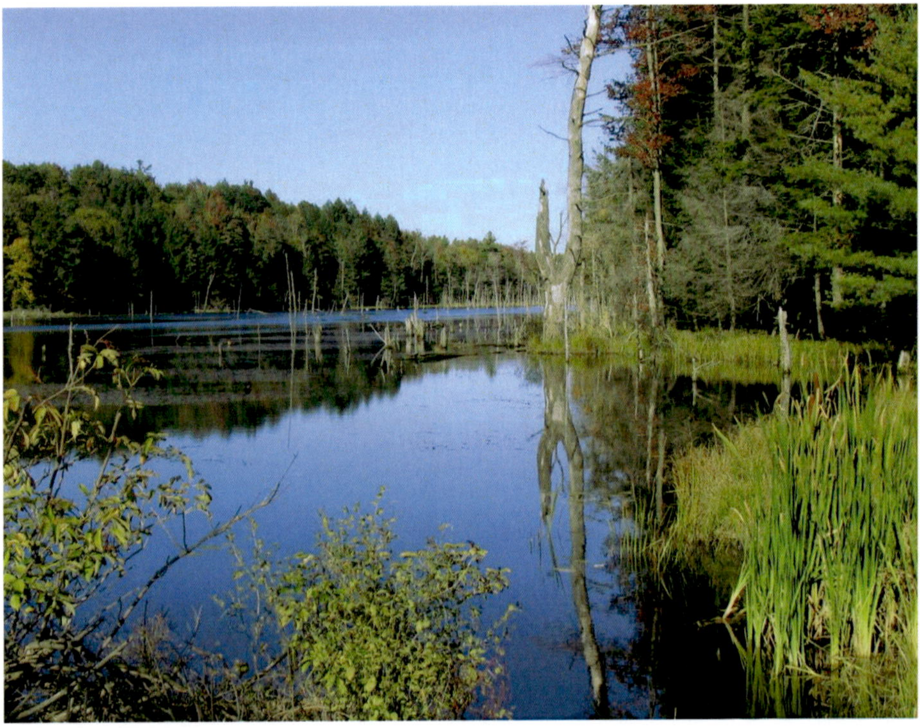

Chapter 32

The Indescribable Tao

The Tao will always remain indescribable.
Though infinitesimal and undifferentiated,
it is the source of everything.
If the leaders of society could harness this source:
Harmony will prevail among all creatures;
Heaven and earth will be in amity;
Rain will gently fall on its own accord;
People be non-interfering;
and all things will follow their natural course spontaneously.
Once the undifferentiated is differentiated into names and forms,
there will be no end to further diversification.
Knowing when to stop, helps avoid trouble.
Like the rivers, which rush back to the sea,
all things merge back into the undifferentiated Tao.

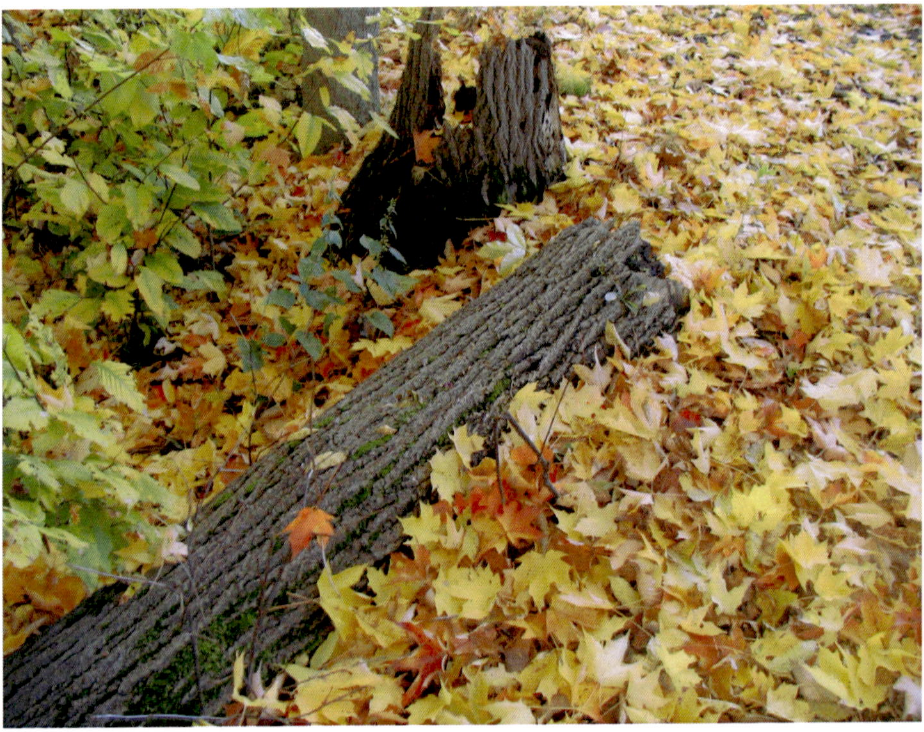

Ashok Kumar Malhotra

Chapter 33

To Die Without Perishing

Wisdom comes from understanding others.
Illumination comes from understanding oneself.
Might comes from overcoming others.
But strength comes from overcoming oneself.
Wealth comes from knowing that you have enough.
Inner resolve comes from firm determination.
Endurance comes from being centered in oneself.
To die without perishing comes from accepting death as a natural event.

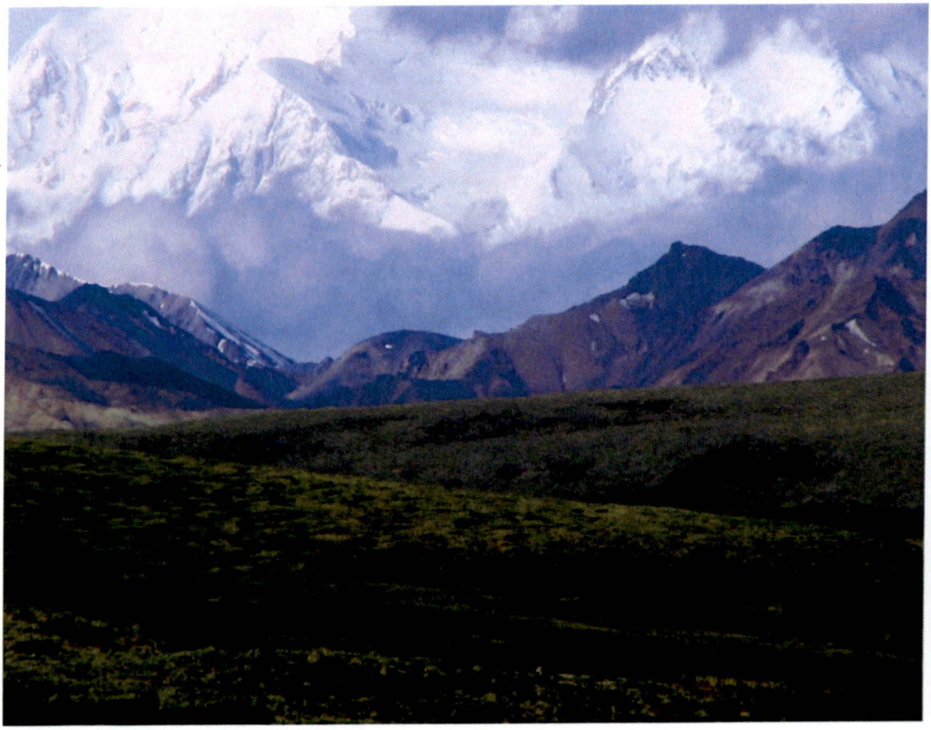

Chapter 34

The Great Tao

The great Tao overflows in all directions.
It is the source of everything
and yet it does not deny nourishment to anything.
It accomplishes its goal quietly
and yet does not ask for recognition.
It shelters and nourishes everything
and yet does not assert its ownership.
Without thought or desire, it may be regarded as small.
Though it is the abode of everything,
it does not declare itself to be their master.
It may be called great.
Because it does not boast about its greatness, it is great.

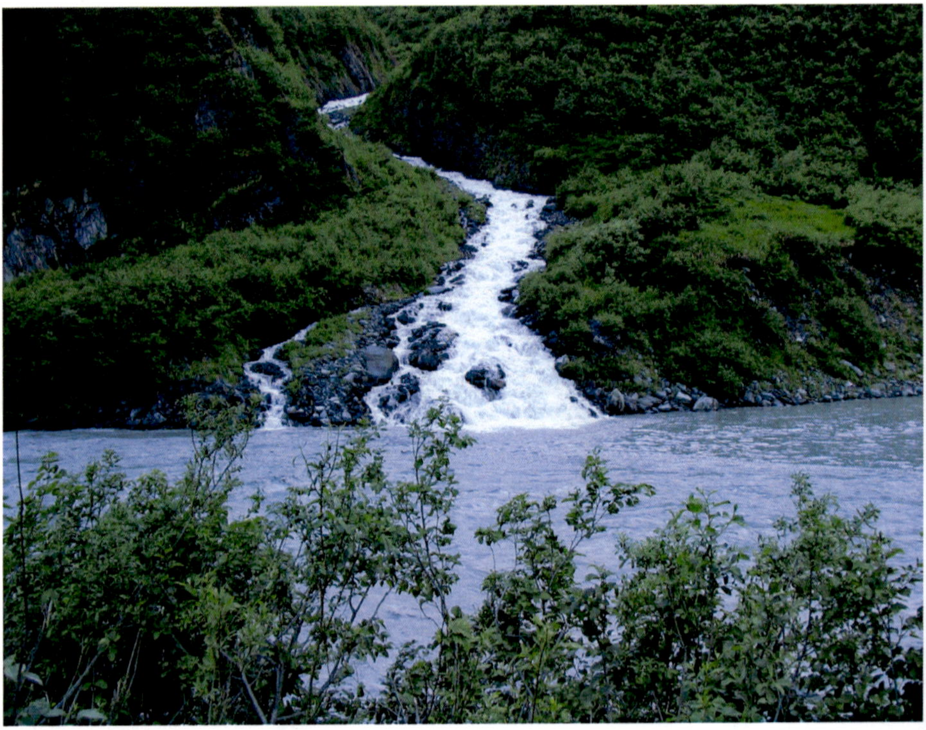

Ashok Kumar Malhotra

Chapter 35

The Inexhaustible Tao

All created beings come to the one (Tao)
for respite, joy and contentment.
Travelers might stop to enjoy
its eternal music and nourishing touch.
But when you attempt to describe the Tao,
it cannot be seen or heard.
But when you try to use it,
it is found to be overflowing abundance.

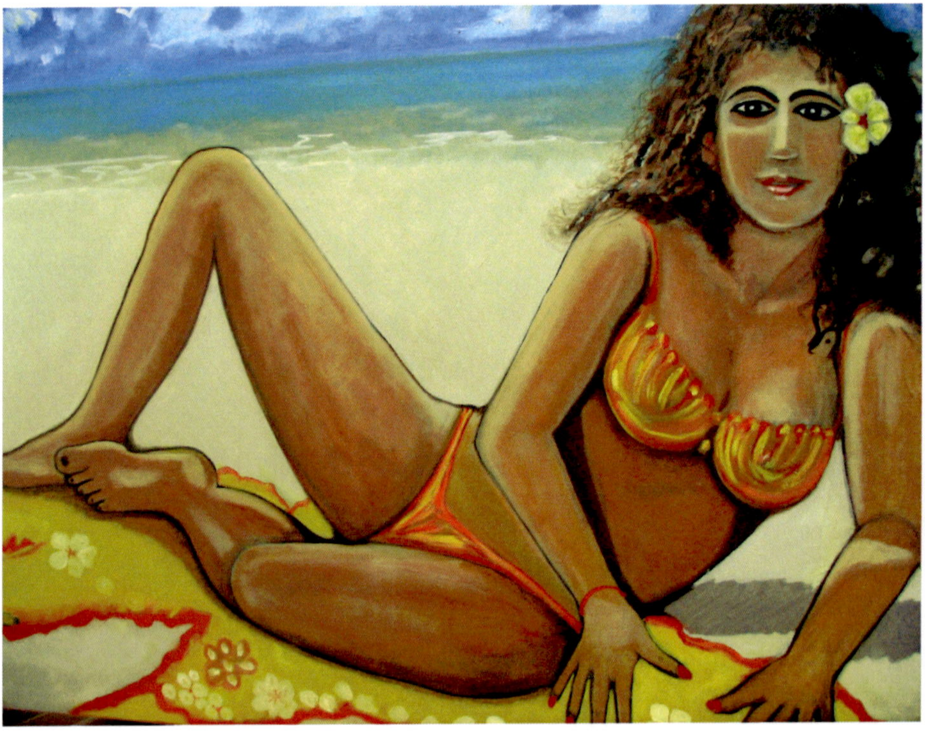

Wisdom of the Tao Te Ching

Chapter 36

Perception of Things

That which is to be deflated must be inflated first.
That which is to be made weak must be made strong first.
That which is to be laid low must be exalted first.
That which is to be taken away must be given away first.
This is the subtle perception about things.
Softness overcomes harshness.
Weakness overcomes strength.
Do not display how you work, but reveal only your achievements!

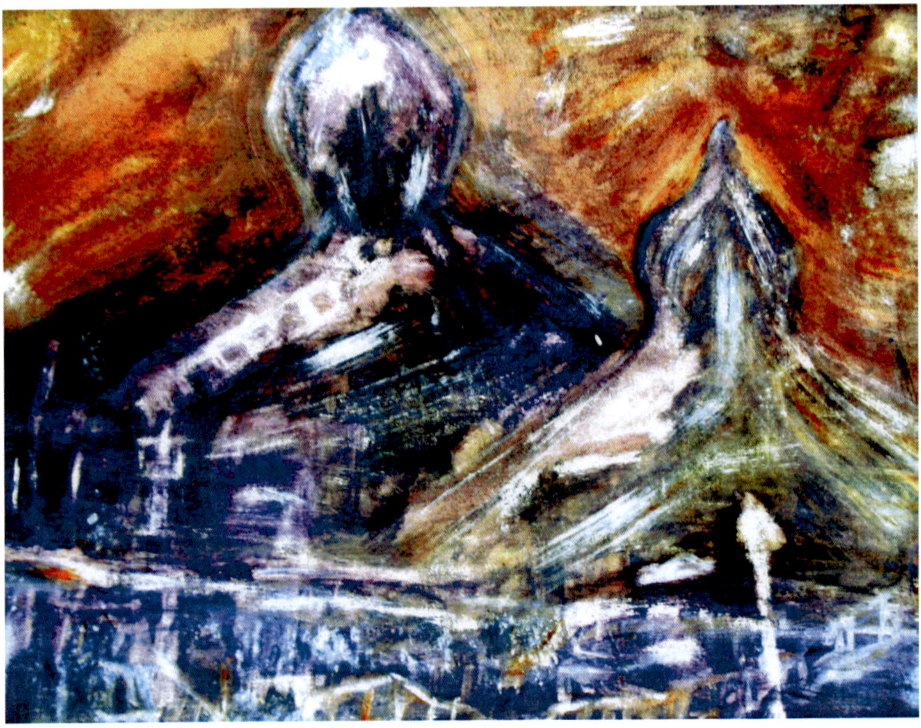

Ashok Kumar Malhotra

Chapter 37

By Doing Nothing, Everything is Done

Tao does nothing and everything is done.
If the powerful men and women attend to the nature of Tao, everything will be refurbished spontaneously.
When people are deprived of desire,
they will be happy, content and live a simple pristine life.
Without seeking, contentment is achieved and the entire universe rests in peace.

Wisdom of the Tao Te Ching

BOOK TWO
(Chapters 38-81)

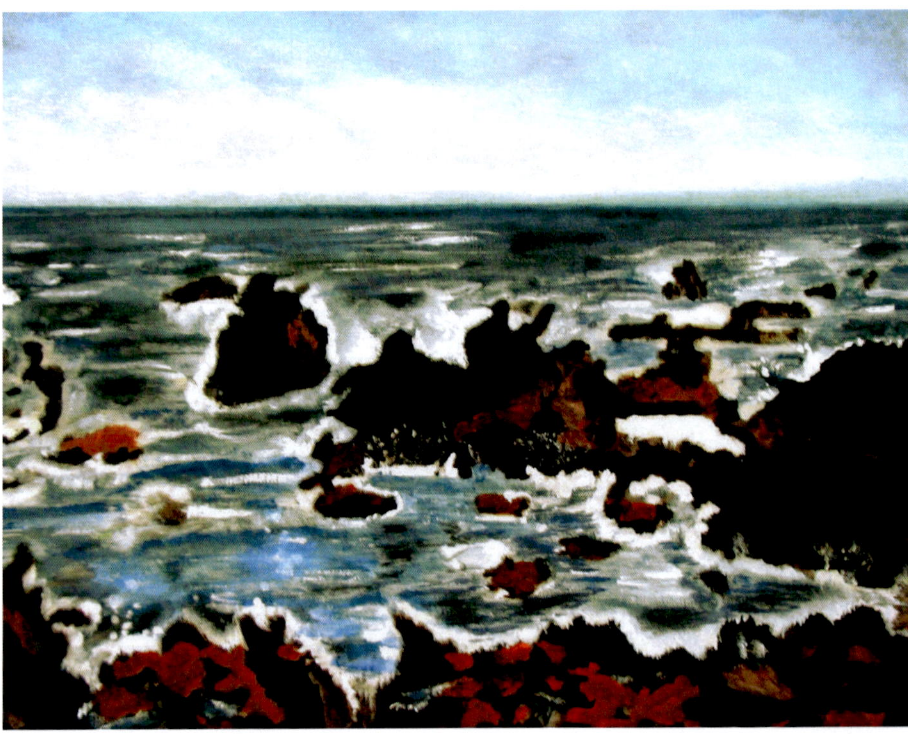

Wisdom of the Tao Te Ching

Chapter 38

Inner Force (*Te*)

A man of higher inner force (*Te*) is unaware of his superiority and therefore is superior.
A man of lower inner force tries to be superior and therefore is not superior.
A man of higher inner force does nothing and nothing remains undone.
A man of lower inner force is constantly doing something and there is much remains to be done.
When a benevolent (*Jen*) man acts,
there is nothing that remains to be done.
When the moral man acts, there is much left to be done.
When a man of propriety (*Li*) acts and gets no response, he becomes an enforcer.
Therefore, when Tao is weakened,
the man of inner force (*Te*) gains ground.
When the inner force (*Te*) dims,
the man of benevolence (*Jen*) takes over.
When benevolence is weakened,
the man of morality takes over.
When morality is weakened, ritual (*Li*) takes over.
When ritual prevails, loyalty and sincerity are dimmed,
so begins confusion and stupidity.
Therefore, the sage abides in the Tao and not in the superficiality of society.
He tastes the fruit and not the flower.
He accepts the one and rejects the other.

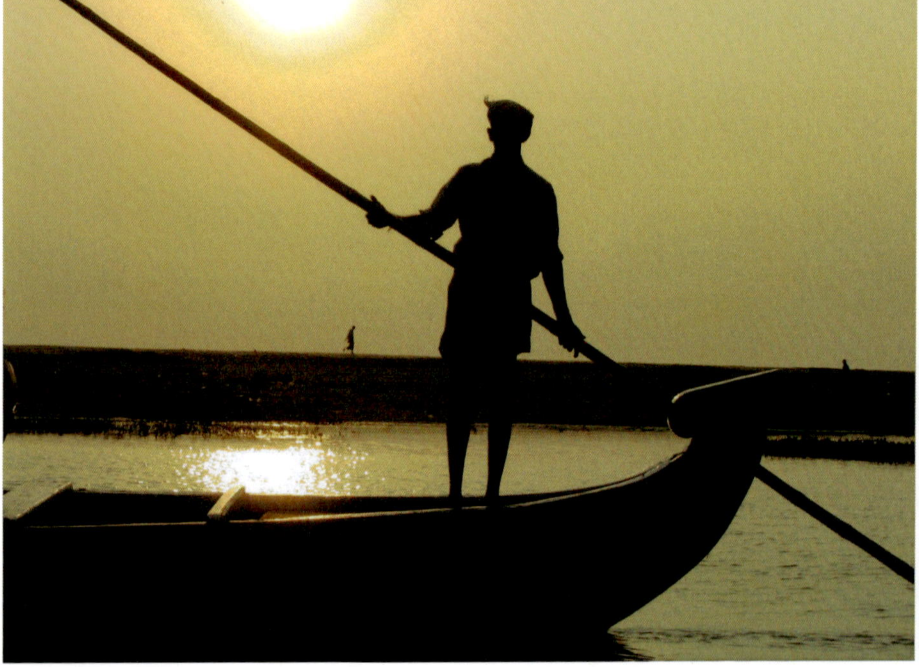

Ashok Kumar Malhotra

Chapter 39

Tao Connection

When in harmony with the Tao,
the sky is vast and clear;
the earth is solid and full;
all created beings are imbued with life
and live in perfect unity.
When not in harmony with the Tao,
the sky loses its clarity;
the earth is depleted of its resources;
the created beings are depressed
and live in disharmony.
The sage understands the connection between the parts and the whole.
The noble needs the humble
and the high requires the low;
just as there can be no chariot without the rim, spoke and the hub.

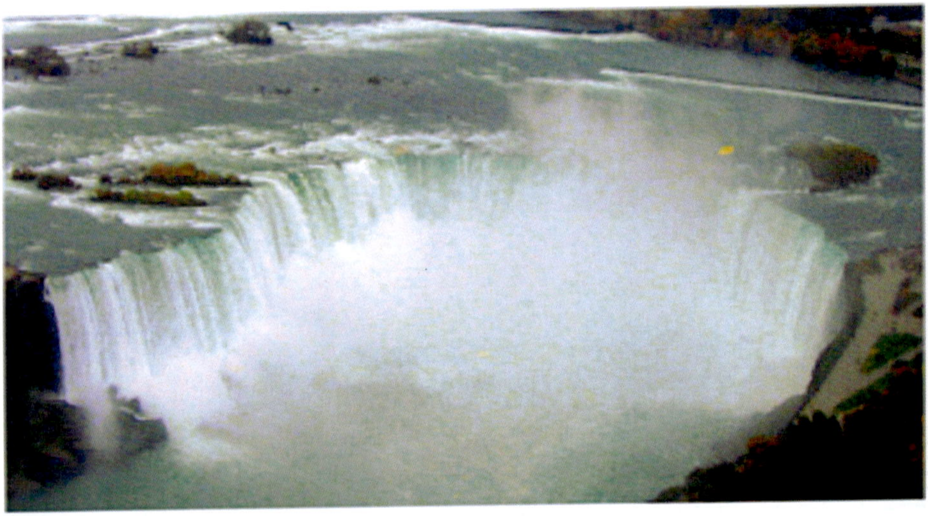

Wisdom of the Tao Te Ching

Chapter 40

The Way

Flowing into itself is the movement of the Tao.
Yielding is the way of the Tao.
Everything comes out of what is.
But what is, is born out of what is not.

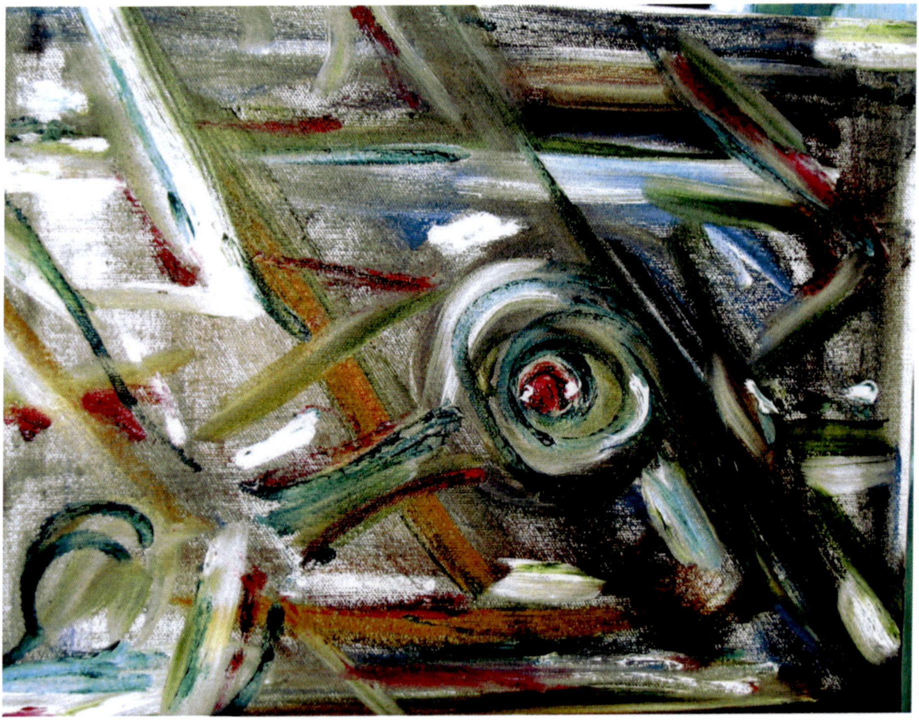

Ashok Kumar Malhotra

Chapter 41

Hearers of the Tao

When the brightest man hears of the Tao, he embraces it fully.
When the mediocre man hears of the Tao, he partially believes it and partly believes it not.
When the dullard hears of the Tao, he makes fun of it.
What will the Tao be if it did not invoke laughter?
To those who embody the Tao:
the path of light appears to be dark;
going forward appears to be going backward;
the straight path seems to be crooked;
the effortless appears to be arduous;
the irreproachable appears to be defiled;
the path of strength appears to be that of weakness;
the immutable truth seems to be mutable;
and the distinct seems to be indistinct.
The perfect square is without corners.
The great talent takes time to mature.
The heavenly music is hard to hear.
The great art is without any form.
The Tao remains nameless and elusive
and yet it is the source that nourishes everything.

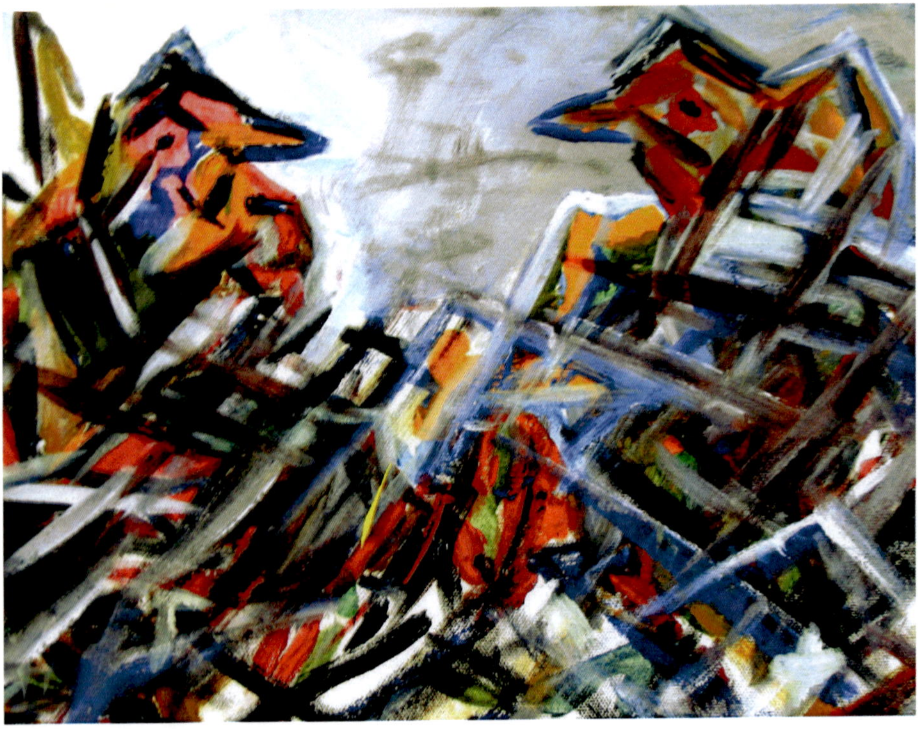

Wisdom of the Tao Te Ching

Chapter 42

Male and Female

The Tao gave birth to one;
one to two;
two to three;
and three produced the multiplicity of things.
The multiplicity of things is embraced and balanced by the forces of female (Yin) and male (Yang).
Ordinary people dread aloneness whereas the sage puts it to perfect use.
By losing he gains and by gaining he loses.
It is when he realizes his solitariness that the sage feels the direct link with the Tao.

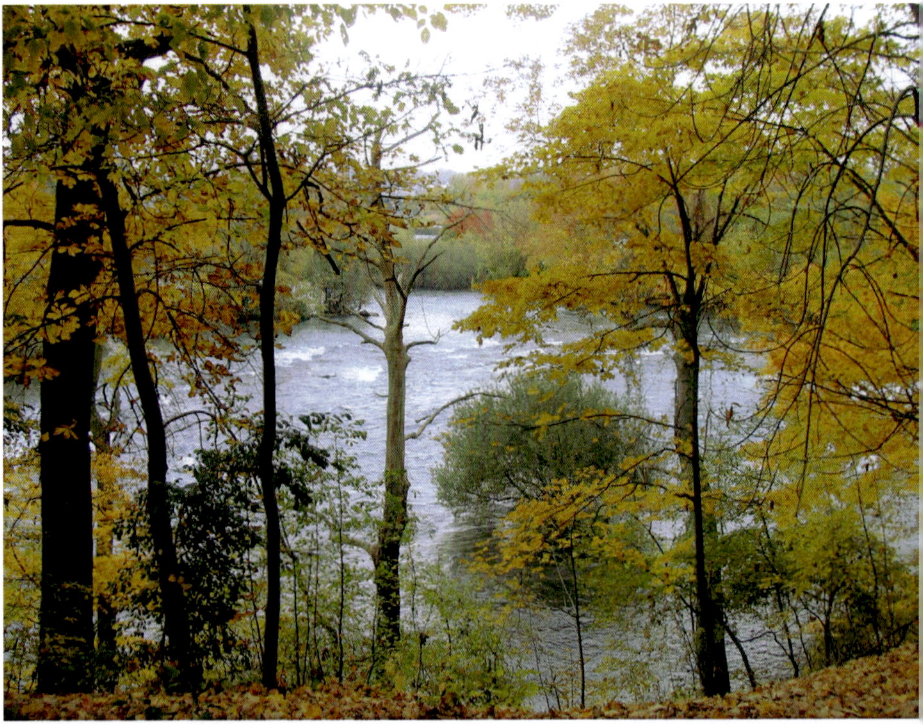

Ashok Kumar Malhotra

Chapter 43

Action of Non-Action

The soft wins over the hard.
The formless pervades all forms.
This shows the truth of non-action.
Teaching without lesson;
accomplishing without action;
this is the way of the sage.

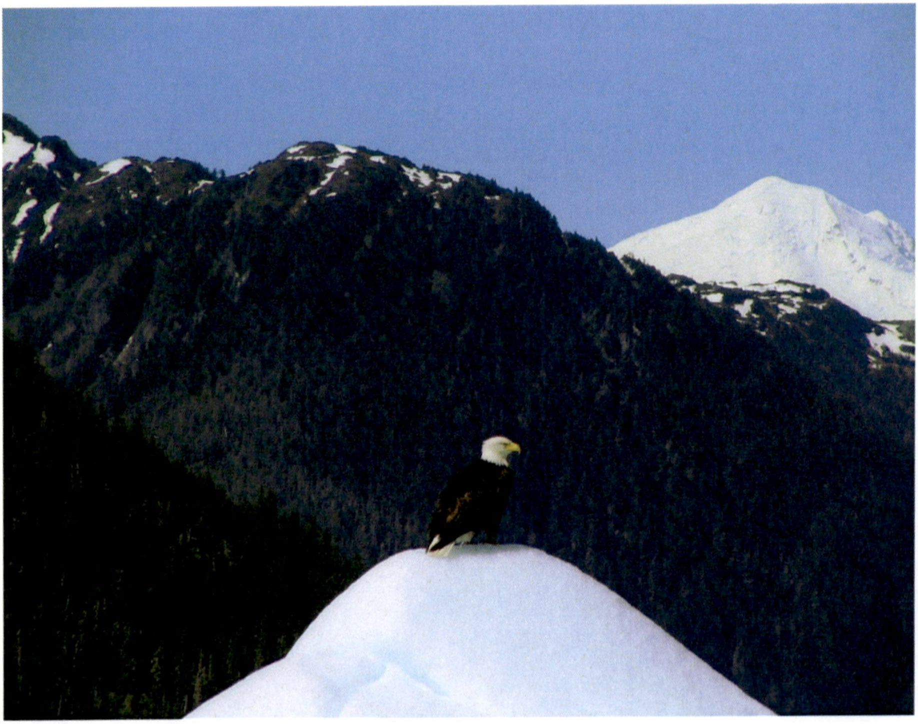

Wisdom of the Tao Te Ching

Chapter 44

To Be Fulfilled

Which is more important: name or self-worth?
Which is more valuable: riches or personhood?
Which is a bigger disaster: loss of wealth or selfhood?
Thus attachment to things invites disaster.
One who possesses much will lose much.
Therefore, a person who is content with 'who one is' and 'what one has,' is fulfilled.

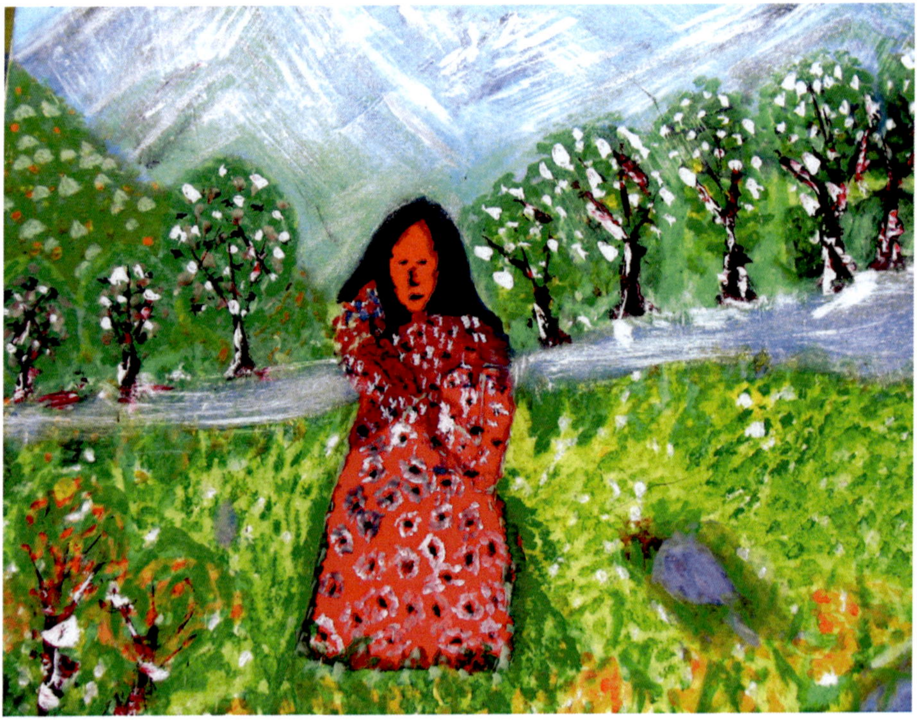

Chapter 45

Let the Tao Work!

The highest perfection is still imperfect
but its usefulness is everlasting.
The greatest realization still lacks something
but its utility is boundless.
The true straightness seems slightly bent.
The highest knowledge seems to be foolishness.
The finest speech seems awkward.
Movement beats cold.
Stillness conquers heat.
The sage stays calm and content and lets the Tao do its work.

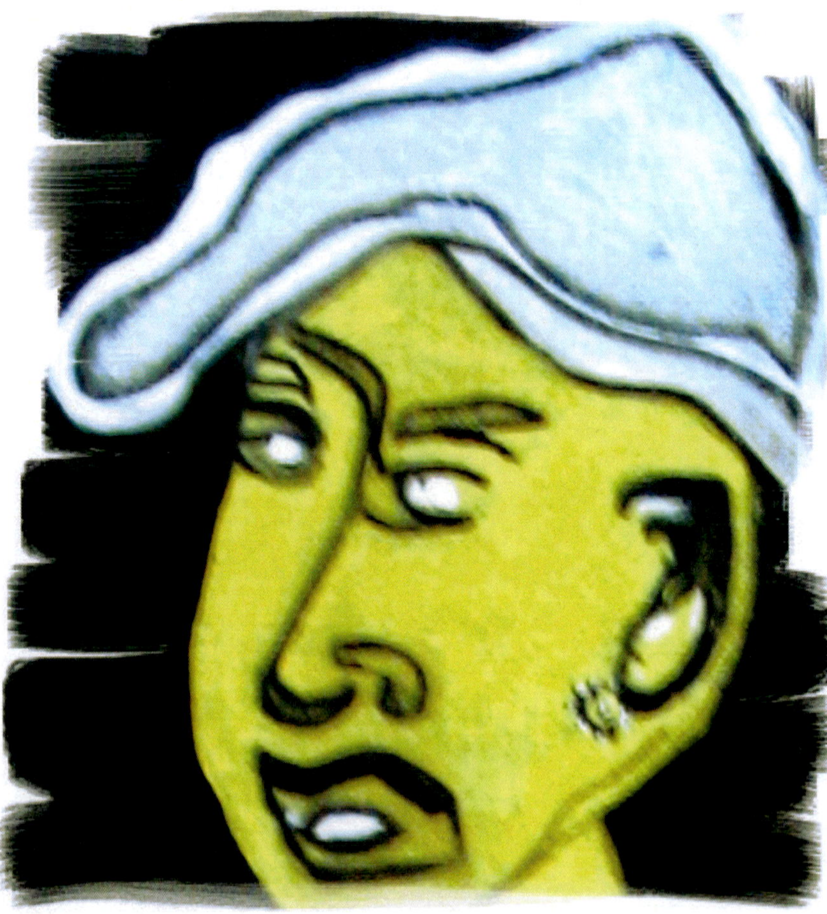

Wisdom of the Tao Te Ching

Chapter 46

Secret of Contentment

When the people go with the flow of the Tao,
Horses will haul the hay.
When the people go against the flow of the Tao,
the horses will be bred for battle and war.
To be discontent is the biggest affliction.
To be attached to possession is the greatest vice.
When you are content with what you have, you will experience true contentment.

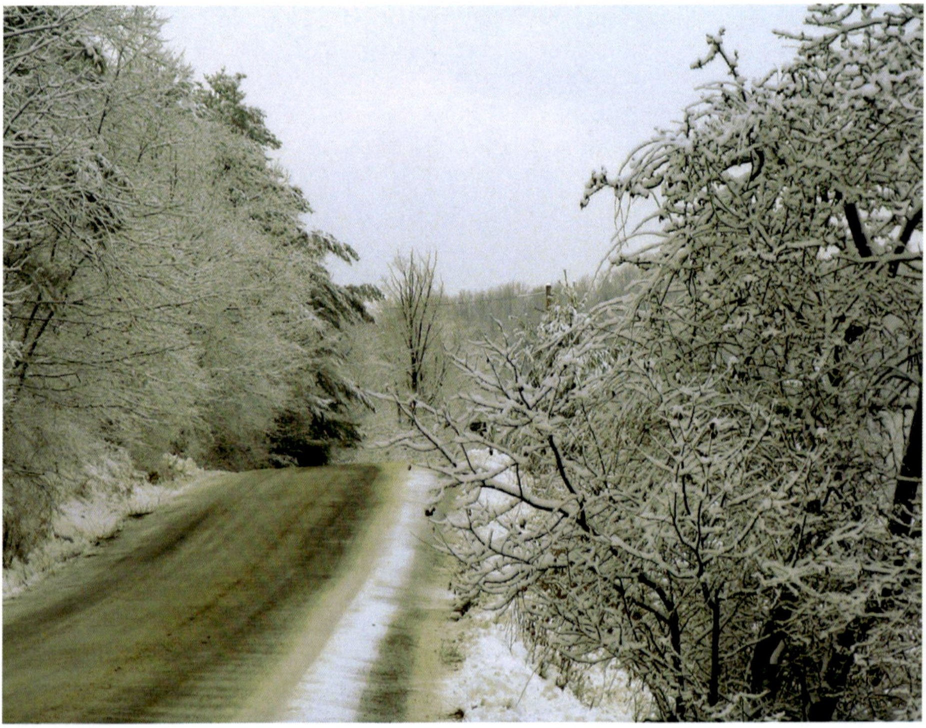

Ashok Kumar Malhotra

Chapter 47

The Nature of Inaction

Without leaving one's home,
one knows the entire universe.
Without looking through the eyes,
one grasps the heaven's way.
The more one travels, the less one knows.
Thus the sage, intuitively comprehends without leaving his home.
He grasps without looking.
He acts without action.

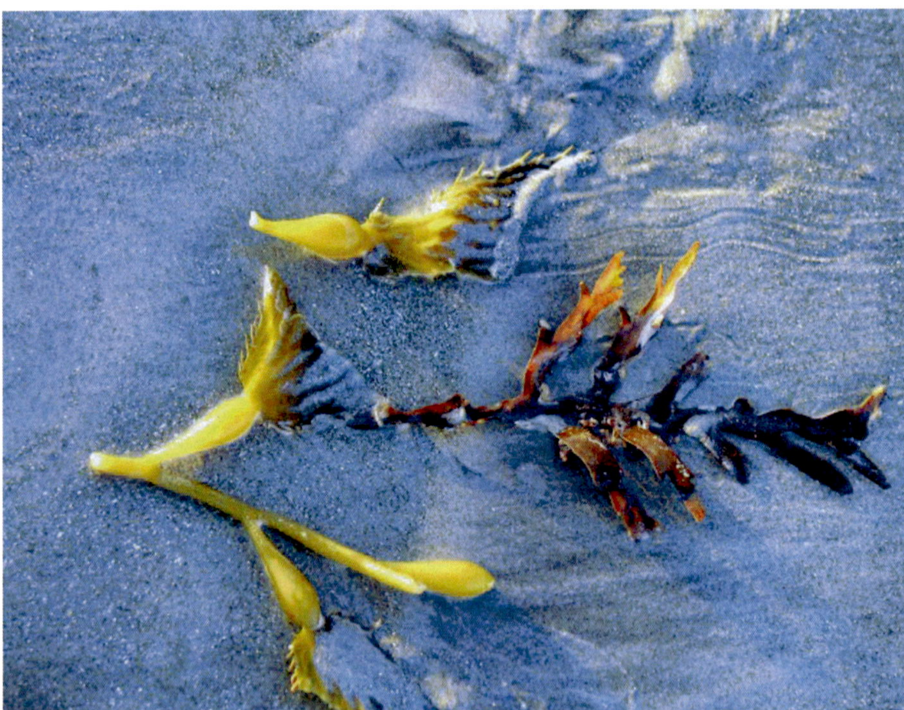

Wisdom of the Tao Te Ching

Chapter 48

Let Things Be

When one pursues knowledge, one fills up one's mind.
When one pursues the Tao, one empties one's mind.
When one does less and less toward turning the course of things, one moves closer and closer to non-action.
When one does nothing then everything is done by the Tao.
The best policy is to let things follow their natural course without interference from human beings.

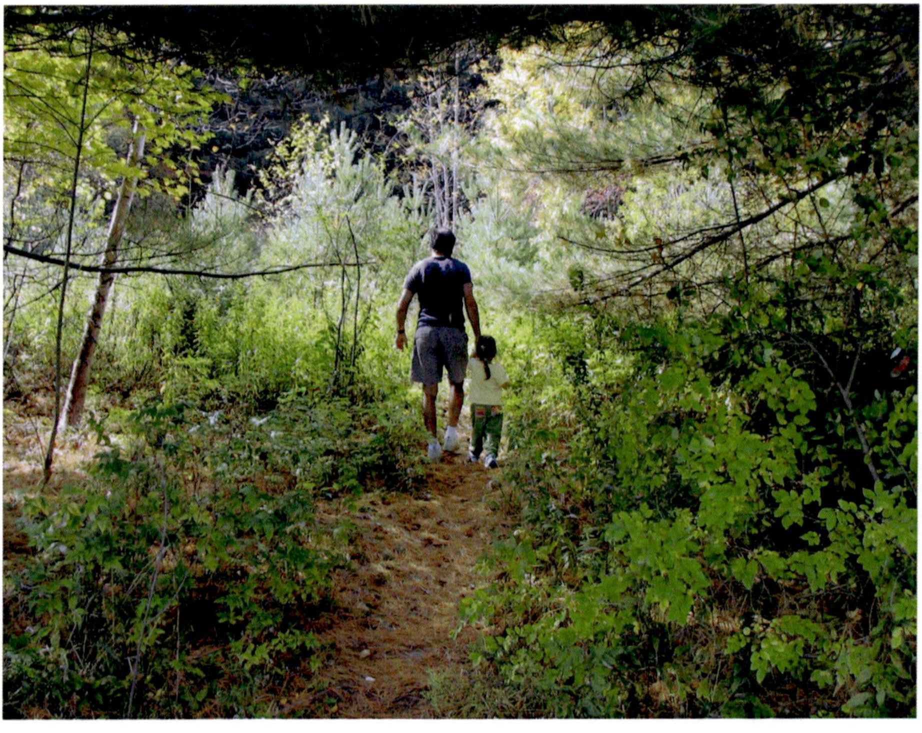

Ashok Kumar Malhotra

Chapter 49

The Sage as a Little Child

Because the sage possesses no mind of his own,
the people's ideas are his own.
If they are good he accepts them
and if they are not good, he accepts them too.
That is the true nature of being good.
If people are trustworthy, he believes them
and if they are not trustworthy, he believes them too.
That is the true nature of trustfulness.
By blending his mind with the mind of the universe, the sage creates unity in the world.
People listen to the sage because he treats them as innocent children.

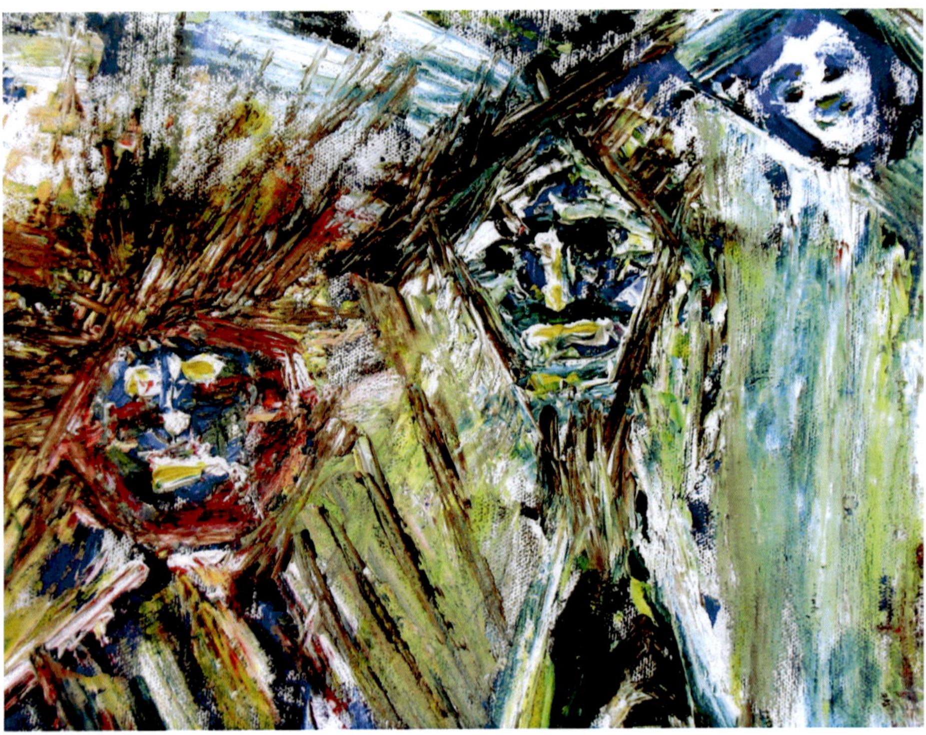

Wisdom of the Tao Te Ching

Chapter 50

Living a Deathless Life

What is the relationship between life and death?
The living human body consists of thirteen organs, four limbs and nine orifices.
Death also involves thirteen organs, four limbs and nine orifices.
Death is the death of these thirteen organs.
Why does death happen to human beings?
Because most people neglect their thirteen organs.
But those who perfect them through exercise by living in the present moment, are not vulnerable to ferocious animals (diseases) or weapons of soldiers.
They become deathless by preserving themselves through vigorous exercise.

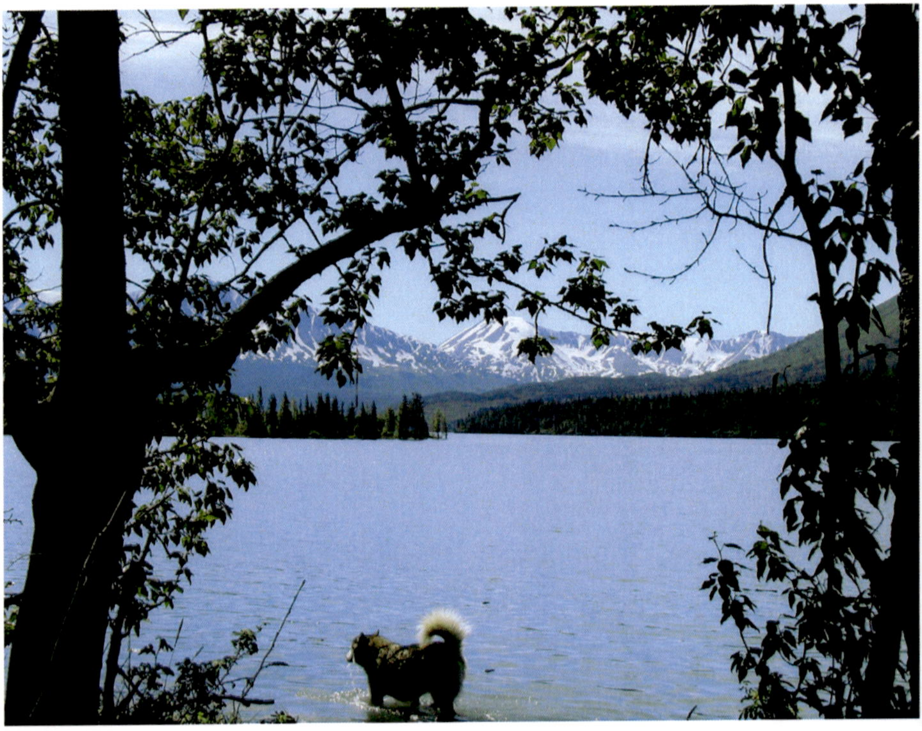

Ashok Kumar Malhotra

Chapter 51

Tao and Te

All things are born of the Tao
and are cared for by the Te.
They are constructed from the material forces
and formed by their unique circumstances.
Thus, all things honor the Tao and revere the Te.
All things are created by the Tao and nourished by the Te.
The Tao helps them in their growth and development,
protects and houses them,
and takes them into its fold at the end.
The Tao creates all things without appropriating them;
acts without claiming credit
and guides without controlling.
That is why everything naturally loves the Tao and reveres the Te.

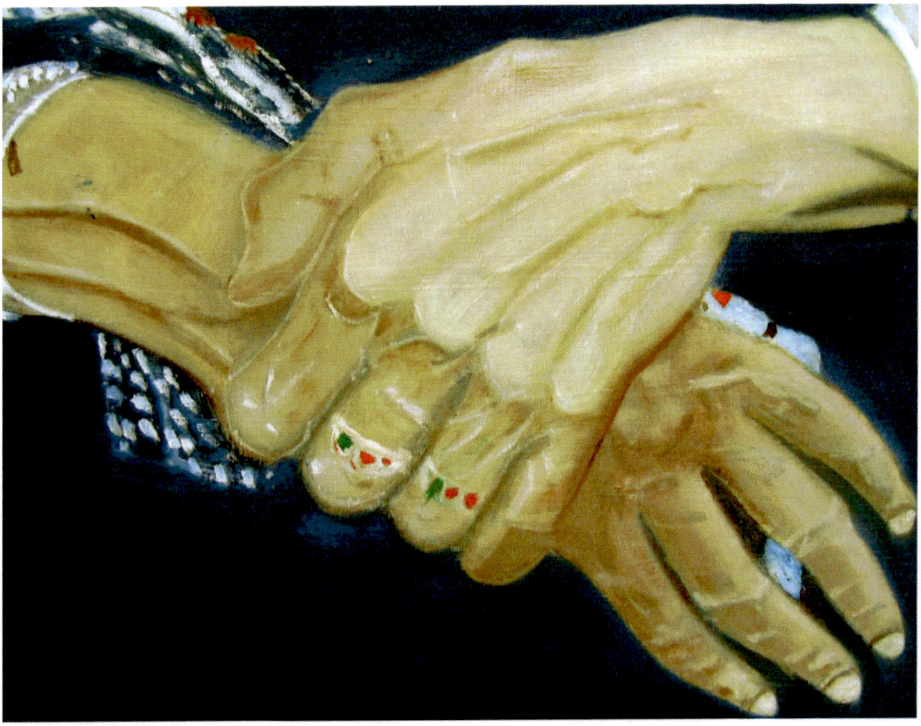

Wisdom of the Tao Te Ching

Chapter 52

The Eternal Mother

The world began from the eternal mother – the Tao.
From the mother are born all things as its children.
When you know the mother, you also understand its children.
When you understand its children, stay closely in touch with the mother.
This understanding wards off all misery in life.
When you control all your senses and desires, you live contentedly in accordance with the flow of the Tao.
When you let loose your senses and desires, you cramp your nature and invite suffering.
When you live a simple life, you have insight.
When you live in gentleness, you have strength.
When you grasp the nature's secret light, you get in touch with the light within.
This is the best cure for all misery because you live in the bosom of the eternal mother.

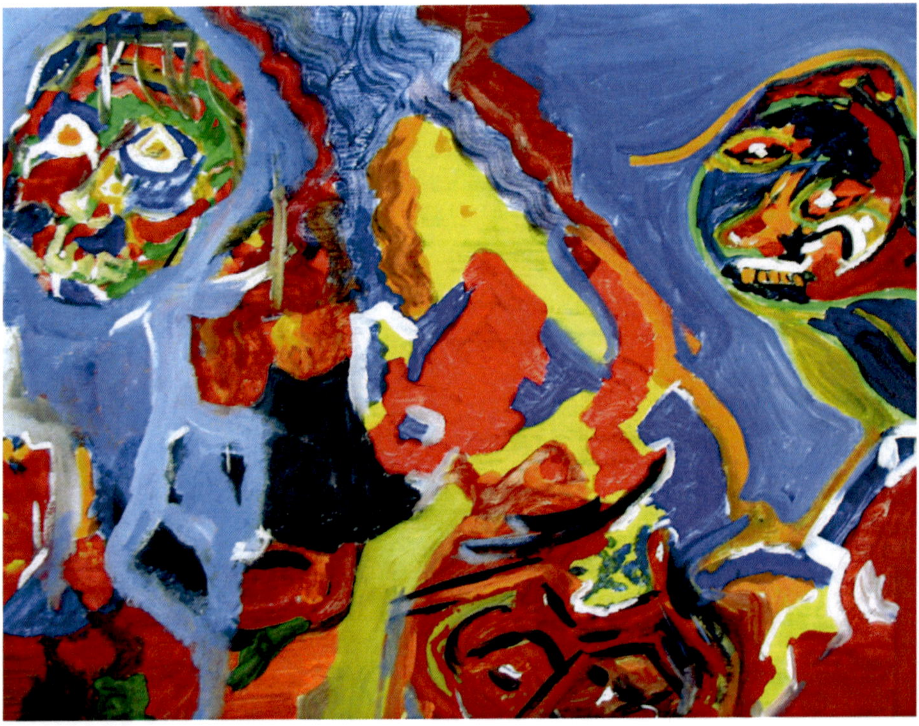

Ashok Kumar Malhotra

Chapter 53

Going Against the Way

You only need common sense to walk on the great way.
Simple and straight is the natural way
yet people choose to walk on the crooked pathways.
The palaces of rich are finely decorated,
while the farms of poor are dilapidated.
The rich delight in their expensive fineries,
while the poor have no food in their granaries.
The rich protect themselves with shining swords,
while consuming abundance of drinks and foods.
The rich go after all the wealth and goods
that they can horde.
These thieves have gone really astray
because they have abandoned the path of the great way.

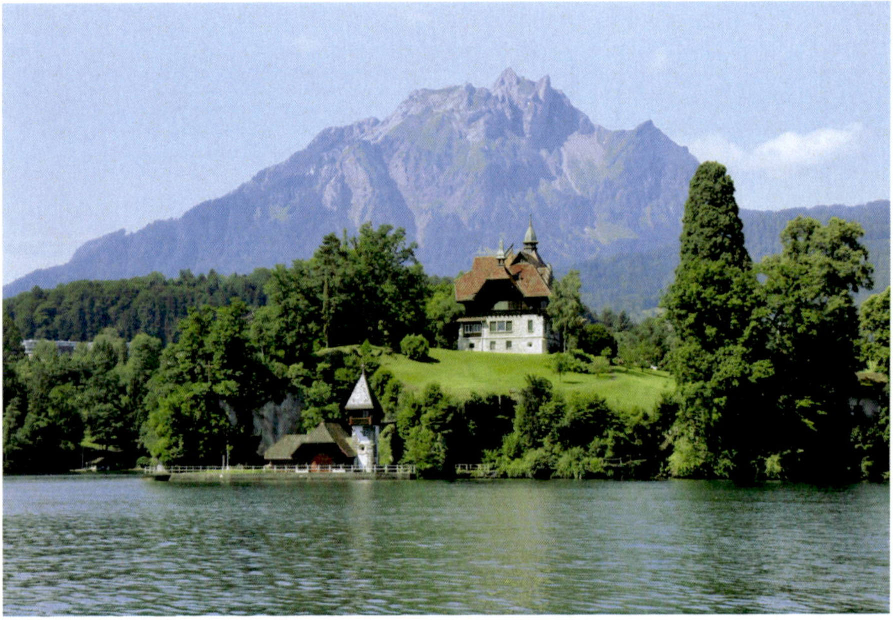

Wisdom of the Tao Te Ching

Chapter 54

Nature of Te

When fully established, your Te cannot be uprooted.
When firmly grasped, your Te cannot be mooted.
Then it will pass on from one generation to the next without any pretext.
When fostered in the individual, the Te becomes unique;
when cultivated in the family, it easily breeds;
when established in the village, it reaches its peak;
when encouraged in the state, it succeeds; and
when nourished in the world, it becomes all-encompassing.
Thus, one should judge an individual as an individual,
a family as a family, a village as a village, a state as a state,
and the world as the world.
How do I know the universe is like this?
Because I am in tune with my inner nature (Te).

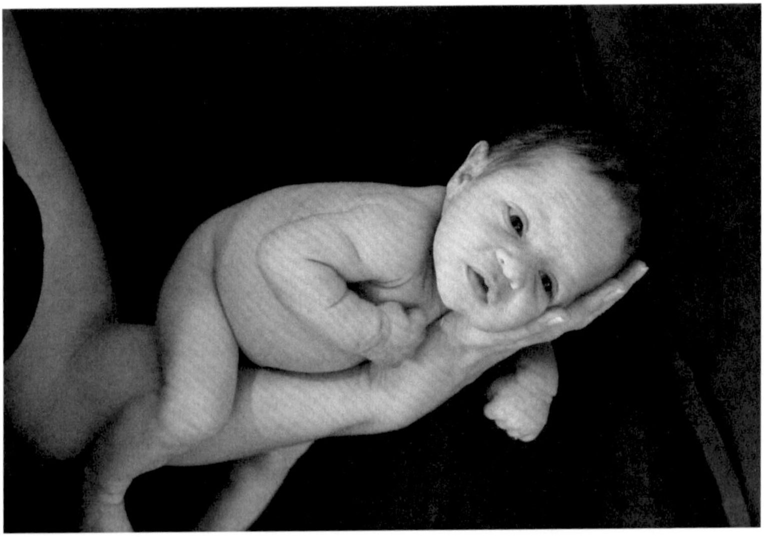

Ashok Kumar Malhotra

Chapter 55

Te and the Child

If you are overflowing with the Te;
you are like a child at play.
You are beyond the stings of poisonous insects;
the wild animals will not regard you their prey.
Your bones are soft and muscles are weak,
yet your grip is firm.
You do not know that you are born of the union of the male and female;
yet you are a complete person filled with all the human potential.
You never become hoarse while you can scream all day,
because you are in total harmony with your inner nature – the Te.

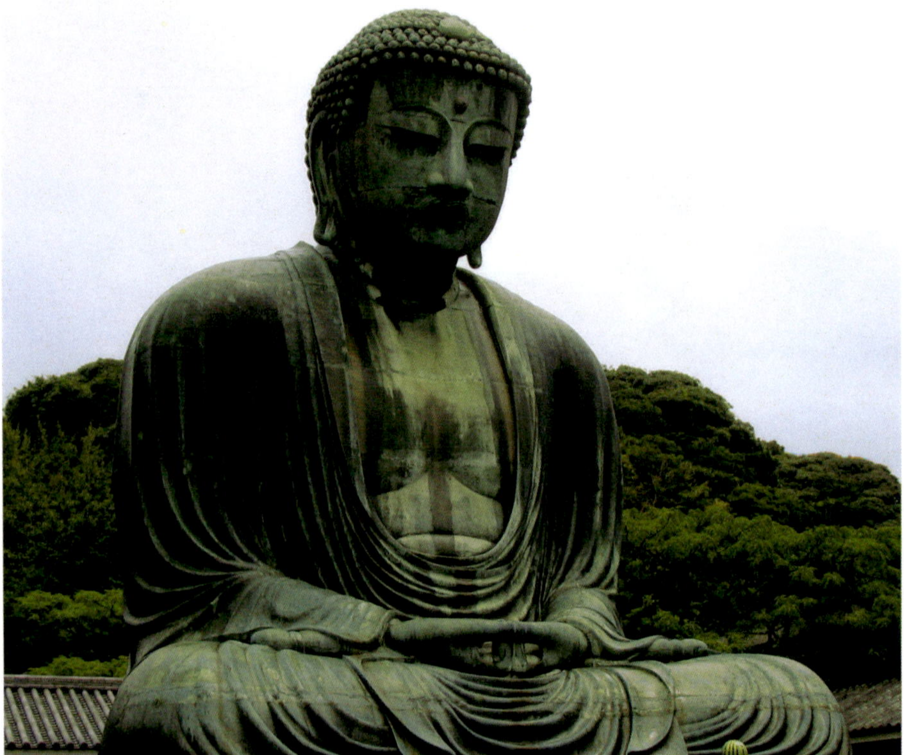

Wisdom of the Tao Te Ching

Chapter 56

Highest Human Being

Those who know do not speak.
Those who speak do not know.
Take control of your speech;
Shut your senses;
Smoothen your edges;
Simplify your complexity;
Hide your shrewdness;
Become part of the dusty earth; and
Realize the natural unity.
Once you attain this harmony,
you are detached from friends and foes;
profit and loss; praise and blame
and have become the highest living human being.

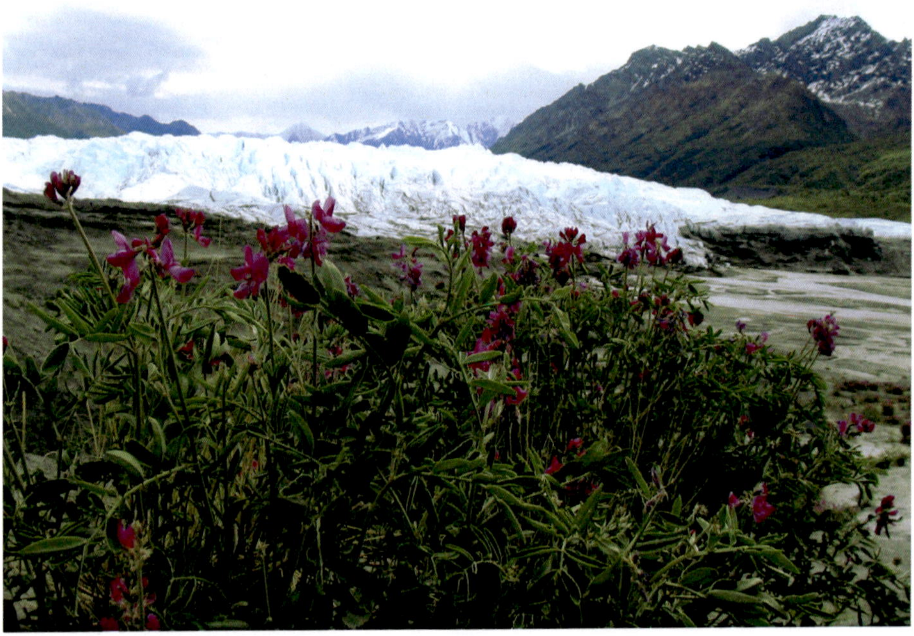

Ashok Kumar Malhotra

Chapter 57

Non-Doing (Wu Wei)

Rule the kingdom through stated laws;
wage the war through trickery;
and gain victory over the universe through non-doing.
Where does this insight come from?
From this:
More you control the people, poorer they become.
More sophisticated the weapons of protection are,
more insecure become the people of the land.
And more laws are created, more astute become the thieves.
Thus says the sage:
I do nothing and people improve themselves.
I am non-interfering and people become conscientious.
I do not demand and people become prosperous.
I expect nothing from them and they become simple and lead a serene life.

-120-

Wisdom of the Tao Te Ching

Chapter 58

Government and People

When the government is non-interfering,
people are relaxed and content.
When the government is interfering,
people are irritated and depressed.
When the government tries to make people happy, it results in unhappiness.
When the government tries to make people upright, it ends up making them vicious.
Who can predict the future?
Thus the sage becomes an example for everyone else to follow:
She leads without impeding;
is one-pointed without disparaging;
and is a shining star without dazzling.

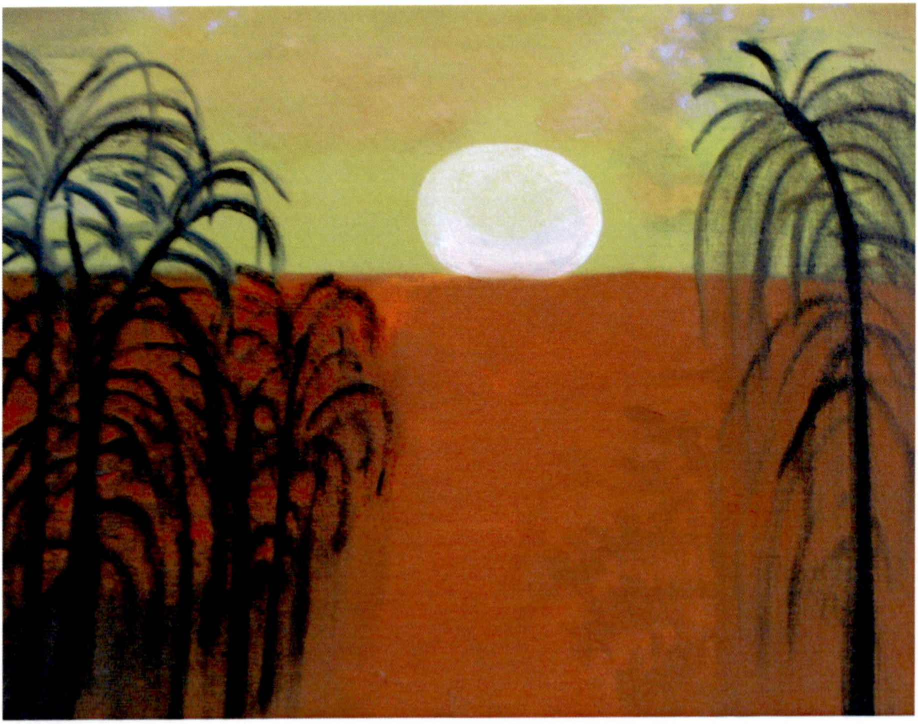

Chapter 59

Moderation

Moderation is necessary to govern.
To be moderate is to be free of presuppositions.
Be accepting like the firmament.
Be all-encompassing like the sunlight.
Be the tower of strength like a mountain.
Be pliable like a tree facing a wind storm.
Be without a fixed goal.
And be like a wandering cloud.
Because the sage is unconstrained and lets go of his ego, everything is possible for him.
He has sympathetic-empathy for all and is like the compassionate mother.

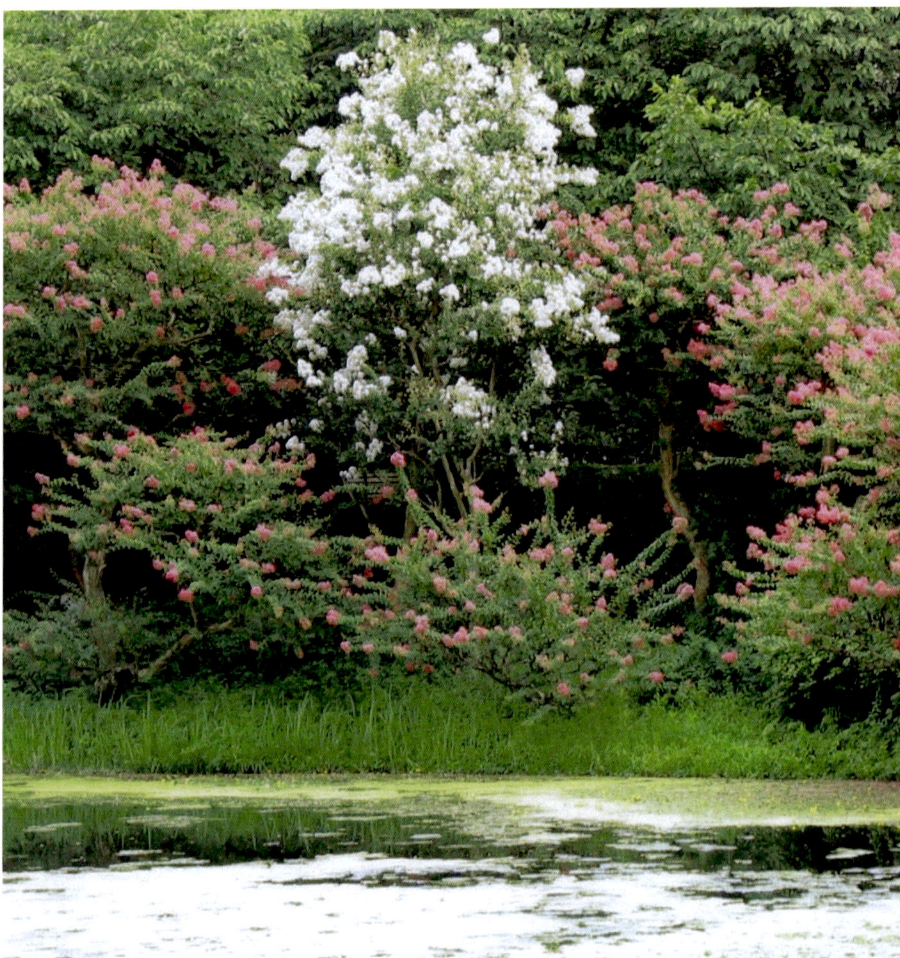

Wisdom of the Tao Te Ching

Chapter 60

Frying a Small Fish

Rule a vast territory like you fry a small fish.
Let the country follow the Tao, so the evil forces will have no sway.
Not that the evil forces have no influence,
the people are not in their way.
Not that the evil forces do not harm, the sage does no harm to people either.
When no one harms the people, the Te works wonders by nurturing everything.

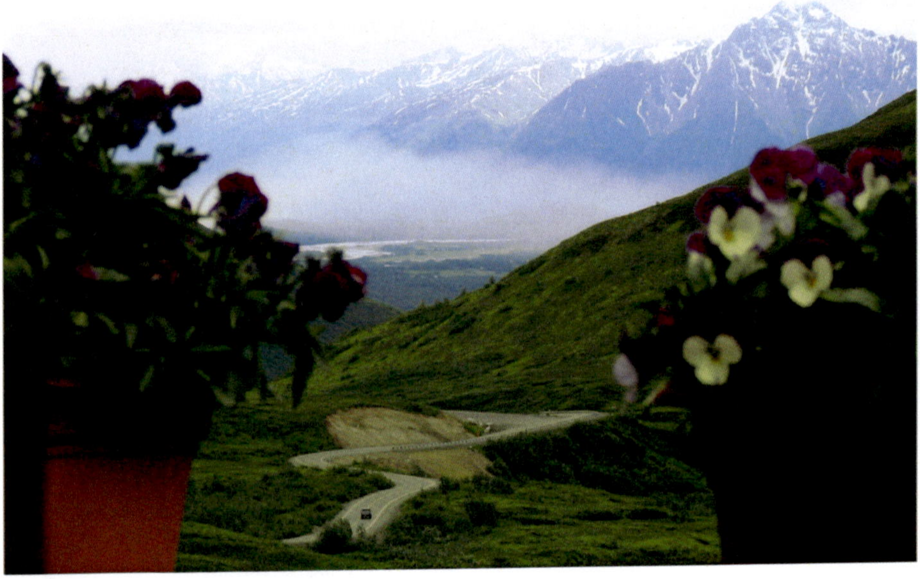

Ashok Kumar Malhotra

Chapter 61

Large and Small Countries

A large country is like a low ground, a meeting place of the universe.
So is the female (yin) that assimilates the male (yang) by lying low.
To win over the smaller country, a large country must lie low.
To win over the large, a small country must yield to the large country.
Those who would be victors must yield and
those who are victorious are so because they yield.
A large country would like to help others
and a small country would like to be helped.
Both achieve their goals through mutuality.
Thus, it is proper for a large country to yield.

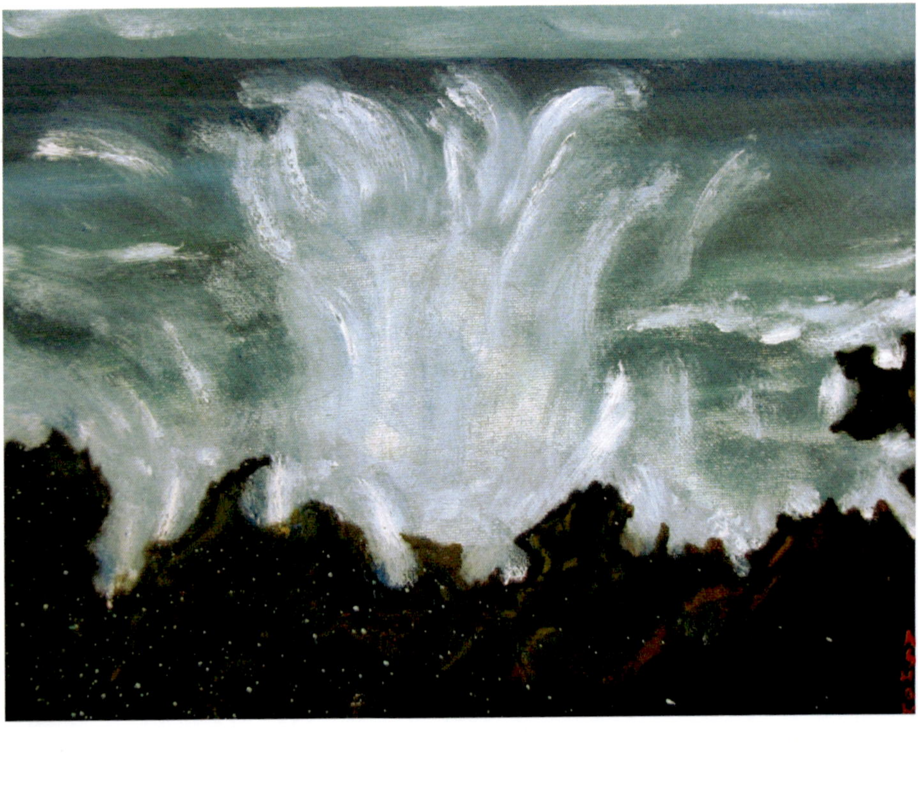

Wisdom of the Tao Te Ching

Chapter 62

The Love of Tao

Tao is the stable source of the universe.
A good man adores it and
a bad man finds shelter in it.
In daily life, a man can fetch fame through good speech
and respect through good deeds.
Though there might be bad men, Tao does not reject them.
People in power should not be showered with expensive gifts
but should be taught the way of the Tao.
Why did the sages of the past revere the Tao?
Because it fulfills people's unique desires and forgives their usual mistakes.
That is why it is loved by all.

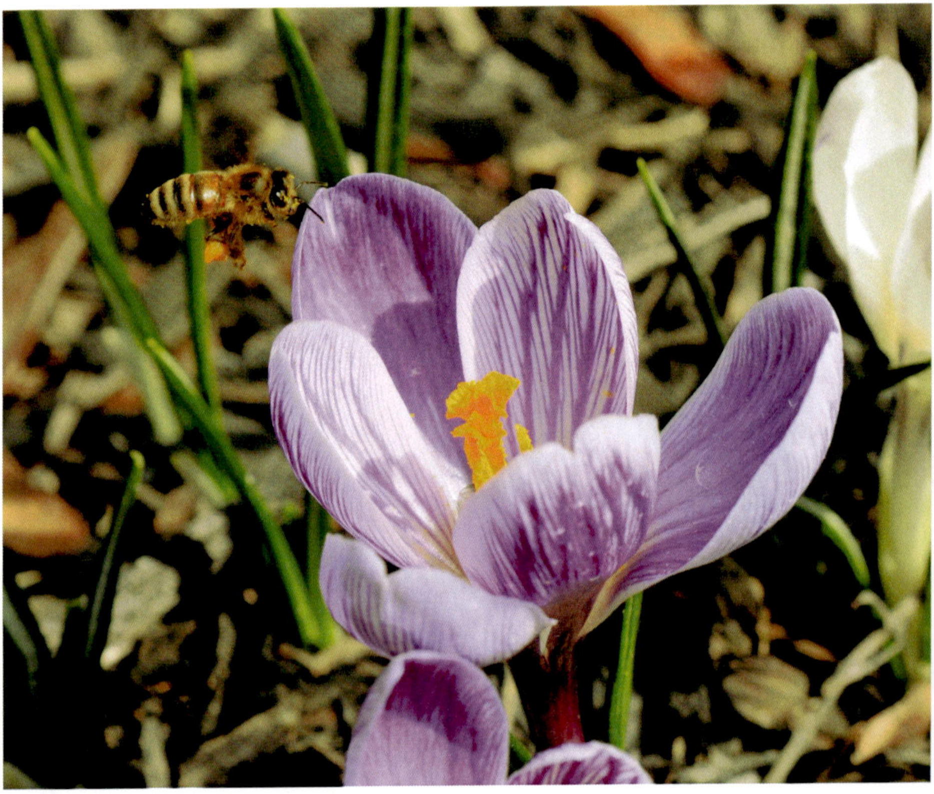

Ashok Kumar Malhotra

Chapter 63

Easy and Difficult

Act without attachment.
Work without effort.
Feel taste in the tasteless.
Be meticulous about doing small tasks because they make up the big task.
Be content with the few things because they make up the big thing.
To deal with something difficult, start with its easy parts.
To accomplish something great put your whole person into doing small things.
Thus the sage does not aspire to do anything great
and therefore does great things.
Those who make promises lightly cannot be trusted.
Those who think everything is easy, face difficulties.
Therefore the sage does not think anything to be easy and thus finds everything to be easy.

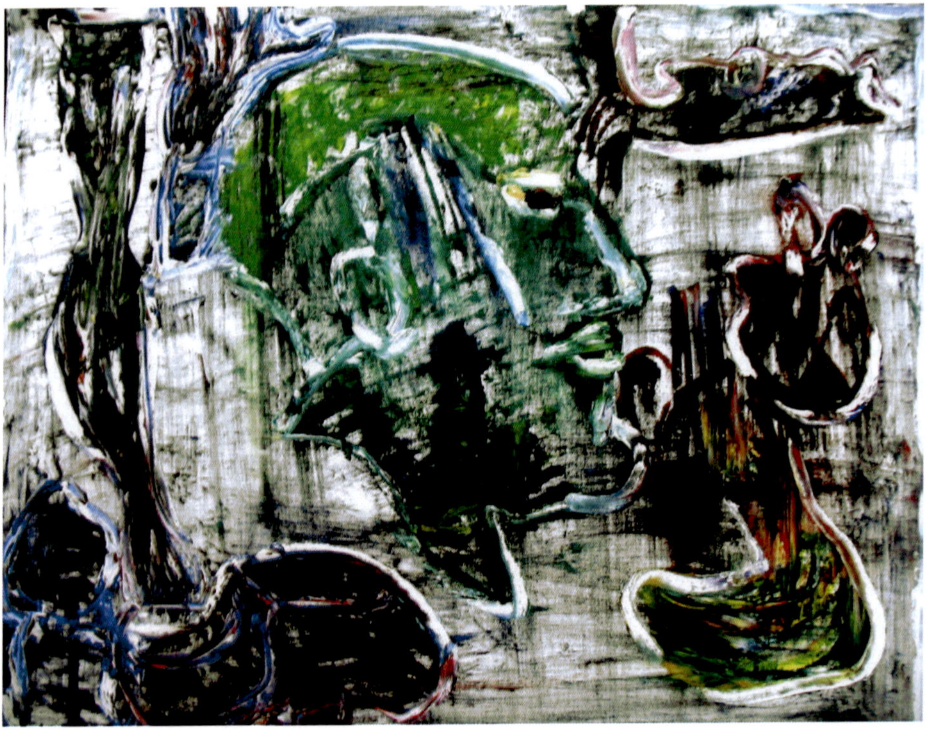

Wisdom of the Tao Te Ching

Chapter 64

Haste Makes Waste

Something stable is easy to handle.
Something budding is easy to predict.
Something brittle is easy to break.
Something minute is easy to spread.
Nip the evil in the bud!
Stop the problem when it is in its nascent stage.
A big tree starts as a tiny plant.
A big building starts with a few stones.
A thousand miles journey (li) begins with the first step.
One who acts in haste, creates waste.
One who tries to grasp quickly, makes mistakes.
Thus, a sage does not act in haste and therefore is successful.
He does not grasp quickly and thus does not make mistakes.
He takes proper care of the end as well as the beginning, and thus circumvents defeat.
A sage is detached from worldly entanglements,
while lacking attachment to valuable objects or to theories;
his life becomes an example for people to imbibe.
By letting things follow the natural course of the Tao, the sage does nothing and everything is done.

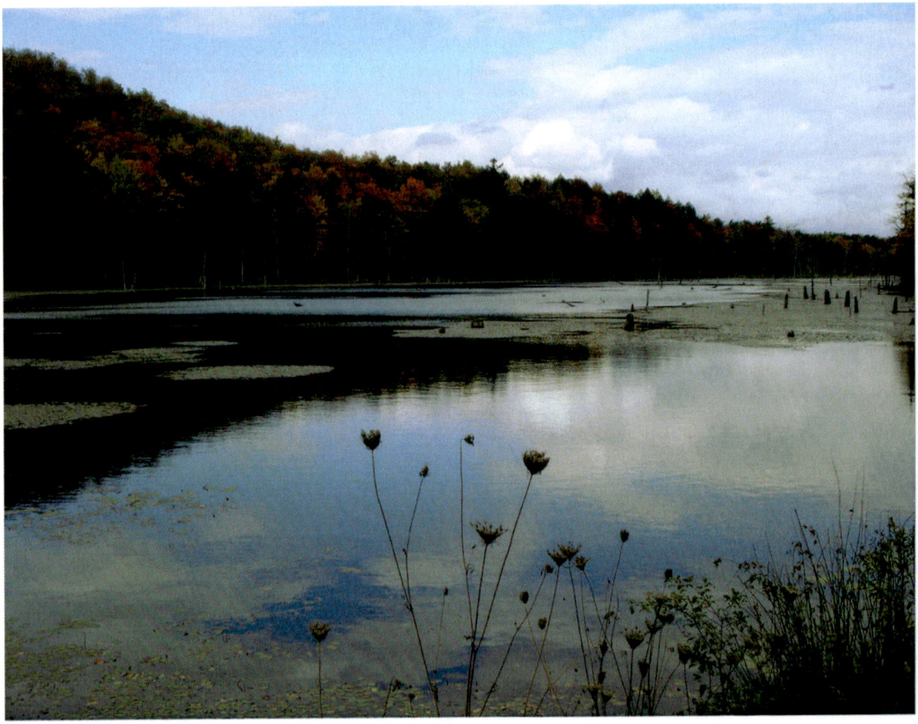

Chapter 65

Harmony

The ancient sages who knew the Tao
did not impart this knowledge to the ordinary people
by keeping them ignorant.
Because when people think they know a lot, they are difficult to rule.
When the rulers think they are shrewd, they ruin the country.
But when the rulers rule without shrewdness, they are a boon to the country.
Knowing these two cardinal principles leads to grasping the pattern underlying the universe.
Thus, this ancient wisdom is the great secret of harmony in the universe.

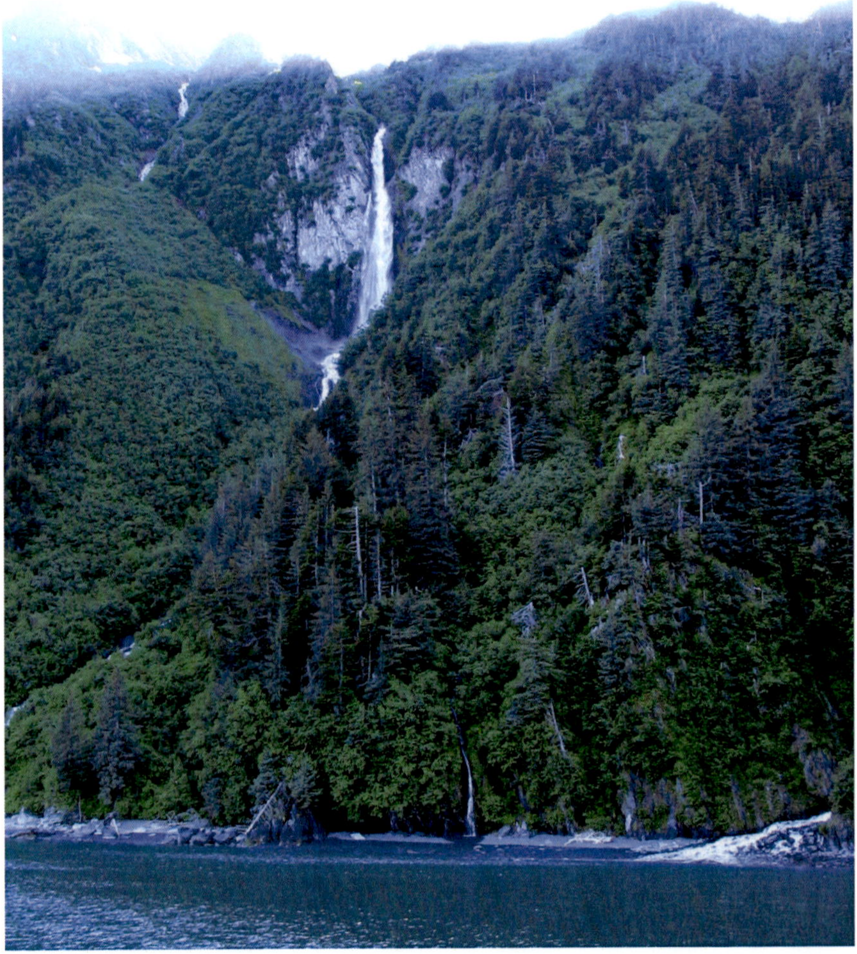

Wisdom of the Tao Te Ching

Chapter 66

Humility

All rivers flow into the ocean because it is lower than them.
That is why the ocean rules over the rivers.
Thus, submissiveness overpowers ruggedness.
To be the mentor of the pack, become the compassionate servant first.
To be the leader, become the follower first.
Being guided by the way, when the sage rules, people do not find him a burden.
When the sage walks with them, they feel safe.
People offer him their helping hand because they feel inspired by him.
Since the sage does not compete, no one feels the need to compete with him.

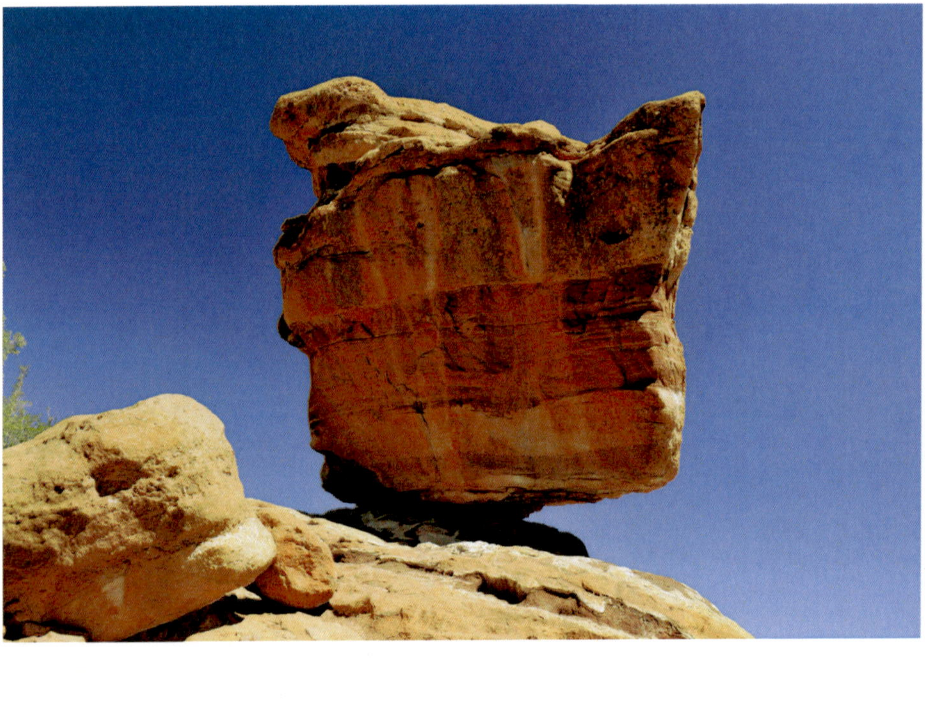

Ashok Kumar Malhotra

Chapter 67

Three Gems

Some say that the teaching of the Tao is for simpletons.
Others find it sublime because it is frivolous.
Had it not been frivolous, it would have vanished long time ago.
This teaching offers three gems of wisdom,
which need to be guarded:
The first is benevolence;
the second is prudence;
and the third is never to put oneself in the first place.
Through benevolence,
one gets connected to all existence.
Through prudence,
one becomes generous toward all.
Through humility,
one becomes the trustworthy leader of all.
Some abandon benevolence
and attempt to get connected to others.
Others abandon prudence
and attempt to be generous.
And some abandon humility
and try to put themselves in the first place.
All of them are doomed.
Since benevolence brings victory in the battle
and is also the best defense,
it is the way of the Tao.

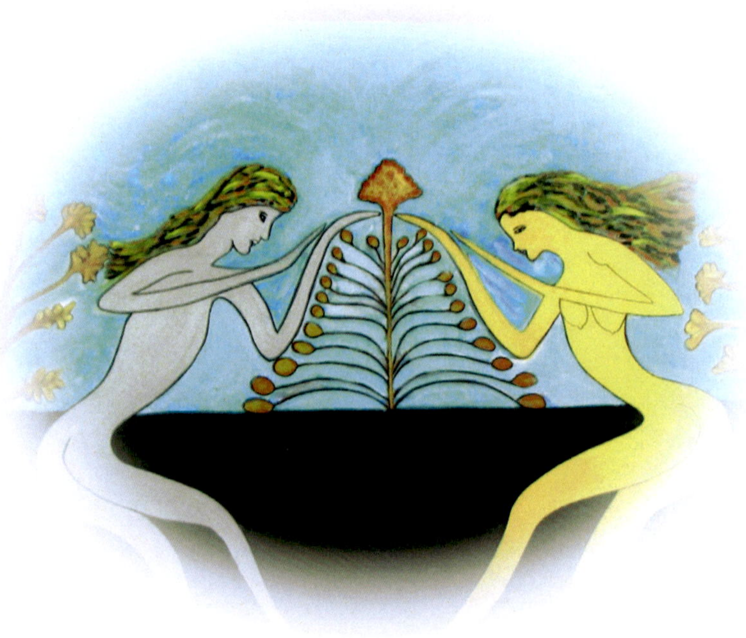

Wisdom of the Tao Te Ching

Chapter 68

Non-Competition

A brave warrior is not violent.
A good fighter does not get angry.
A victorious general is not malicious.
A great leader is a servant of the people.
This is the wisdom of non-competition.
This is the best way to lead people.
This is the lofty way of the Tao
that brings out the best in each created being.

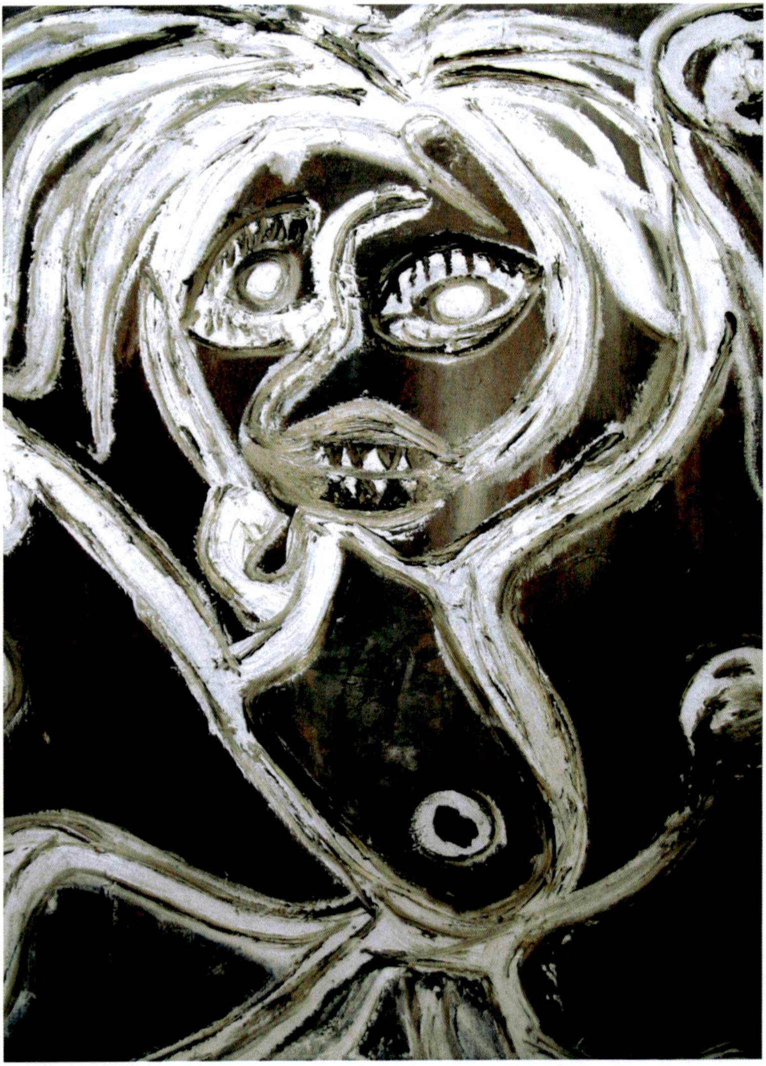

Ashok Kumar Malhotra

Chapter 69

The Underdog

The army's sayings of victory:
I attack only when I am invaded;
I retreat a foot in order to gain an inch;
I move ahead without going forward;
I am prepared to fight without being belligerent;
Thus, I am armed without weapons.
The army's sayings of defeat:
The enemy is ill-prepared;
Thus, the enemy cannot defeat me.
Therefore, when two equally strong armies face each other, success will belong to the underdog.

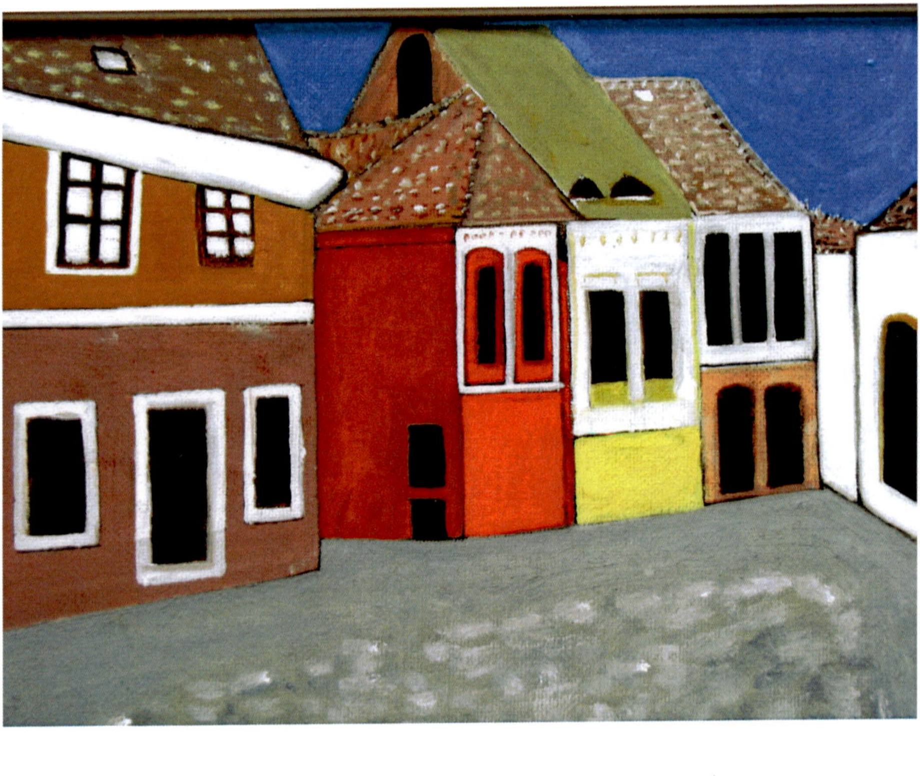

Wisdom of the Tao Te Ching

Chapter 70

Simple Teaching

My ideas are simple to grasp and easy to practice.
But no one understands them or practices them.
This teaching originated in the ancient times.
This practice was started by the venerable masters.
Those who do not grasp this do not understand me.
Since very few comprehend my teaching,
I feel honored.
Thus the sage who wears a strange attire carries this knowledge in his heart.

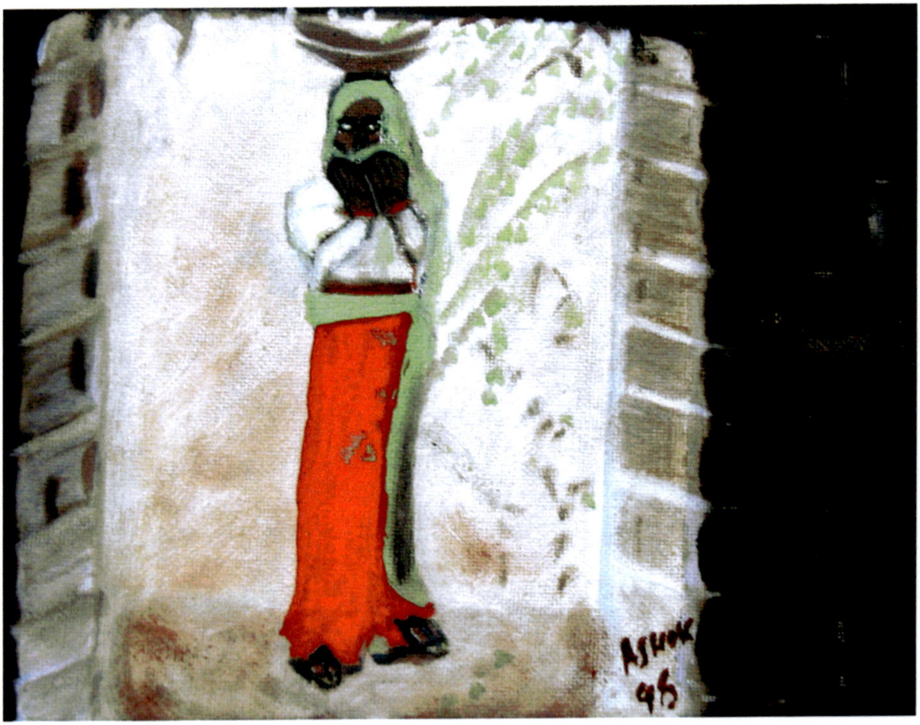
ASHOK

Ashok Kumar Malhotra

Chapter 71

Know by Knowing Nothing

One who knows that he knows nothing really knows.
One who pretends that he knows is sick.
One who knows sickness as sickness is free of sickness.
The sage is not sick because he knows that he is sick of sickness, and therefore he is not sick.

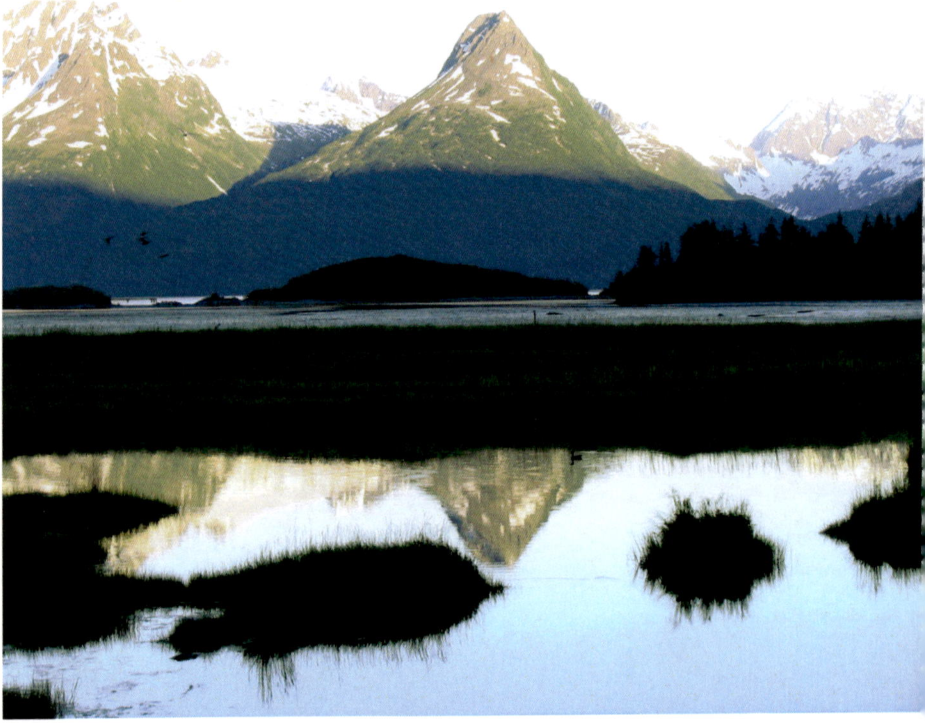

Wisdom of the Tao Te Ching

Chapter 72

The Force

When people are not scared of force,
it will descend on them.
Do not force a life-style on people or their family!
If you do not tire them, they will not be tired of you.
Thus, a sage knows his uniqueness
but does not ask for recognition.
He respects himself without deifying himself.
He accepts one and rejects the other.

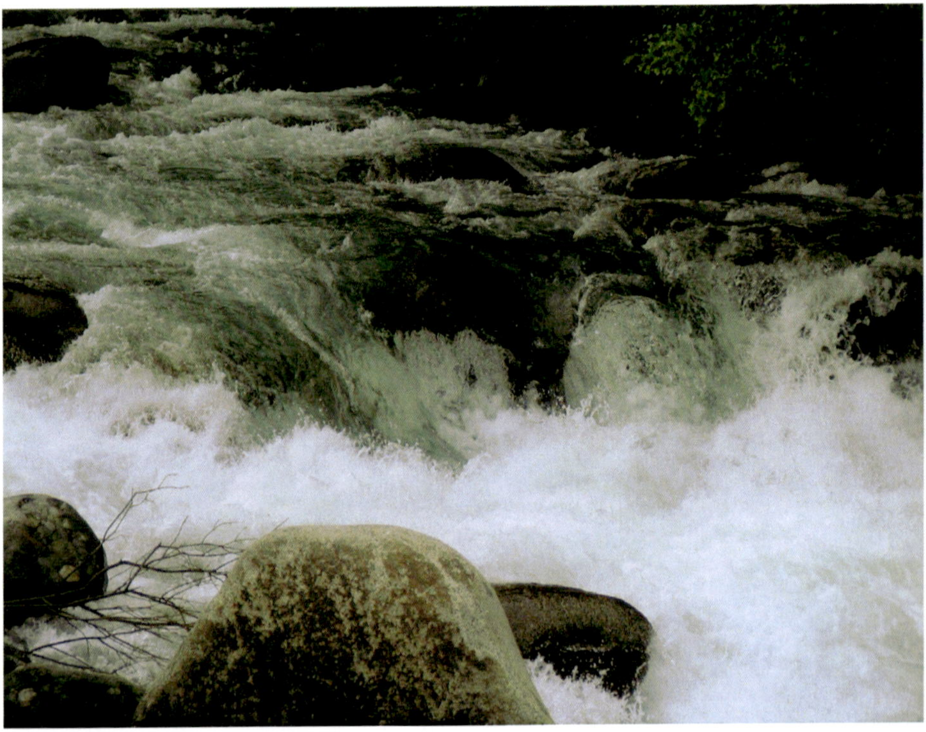

Ashok Kumar Malhotra

Chapter 73

Tao's Web

One who foolishly uses his bravery, destroys.
One who wisely uses his bravery, saves.
Heaven is neutral toward the two!
Who knows why?
The way of the Tao is simple.
Without competing, it overcomes.
Without speaking, it responds.
Without being called, it appears.
Without any plan, it offers a great design.
From the encompassing web of the Tao, though loosely connected, nothing escapes.

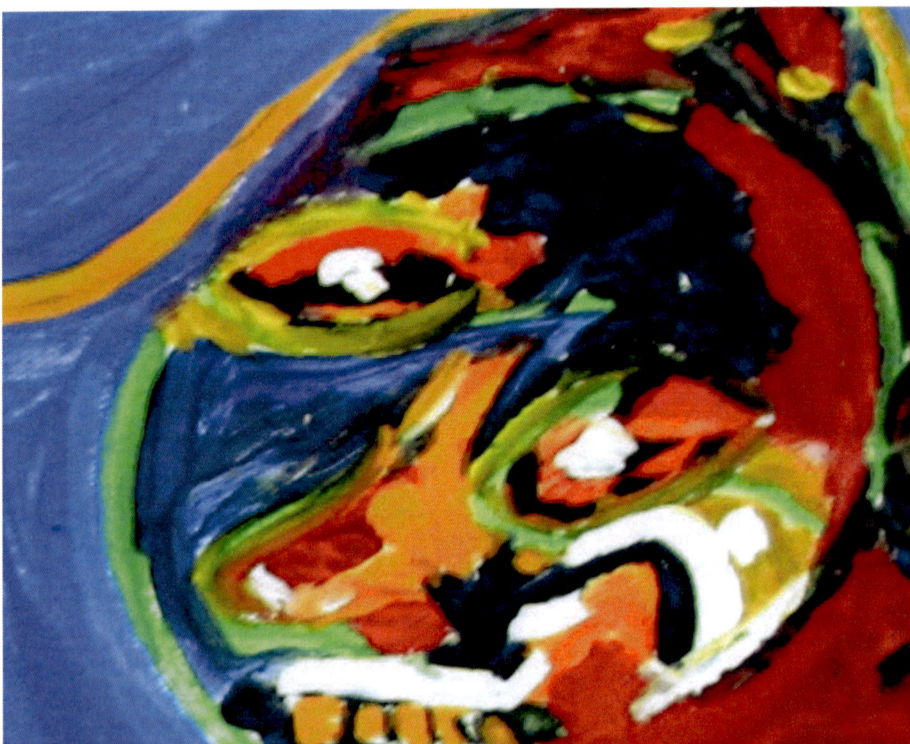

Wisdom of the Tao Te Ching

Chapter 74

Death

One who is not afraid of dying,
death does not frighten him.
One who is afraid of dying,
the fear of death will be a deterrent to doing evil deeds.
Leave all execution to nature!
When one tries to imitate the master executioner,
one will certainly inflict injury on oneself.

-154-

Chapter 75

Government

When overtaxed by the government, people go hungry.
When too restricted by the government, people rebel.
When deprived of living a dignified life, people are not afraid of dying.
Therefore, the wise rulers revere life by letting people live their own lives.

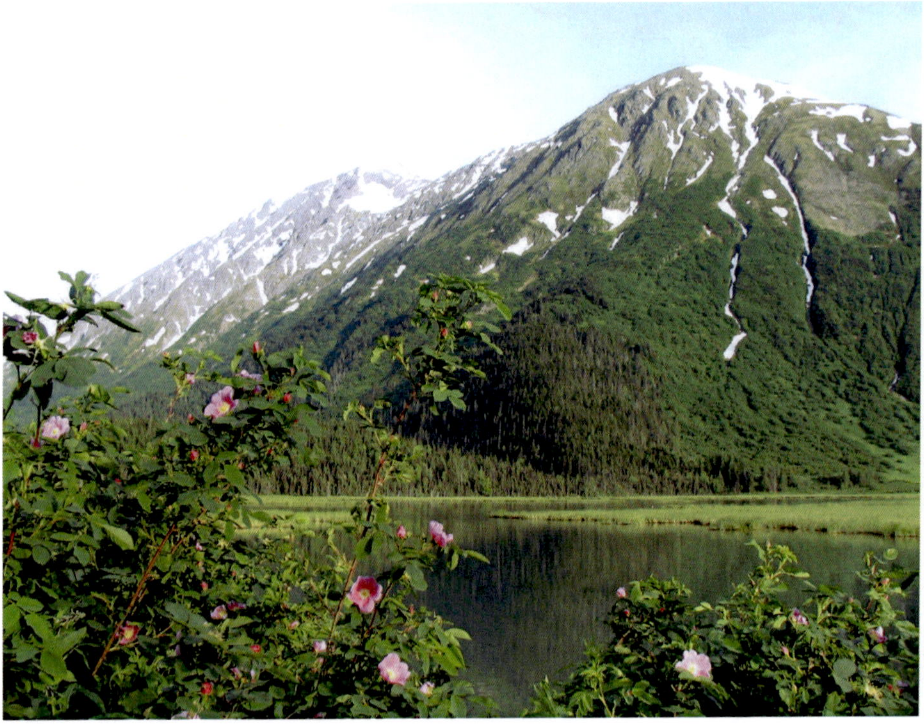

Wisdom of the Tao Te Ching

Chapter 76

Life and Death

When a human being is born, it is delicate and pliable.
When a human being is dead, it is hard and rigid.
When plants are born, they are green and bendable.
When they are dead, they are dry and brittle.
All those who are hard and stiff are messengers of death.
All those who are soft and pliable are messengers of life.
An unbending army is sure to be defeated.
An unbending tree is certain to be uprooted.
All that is hard and stiff will die and all that is soft and pliable will survive.

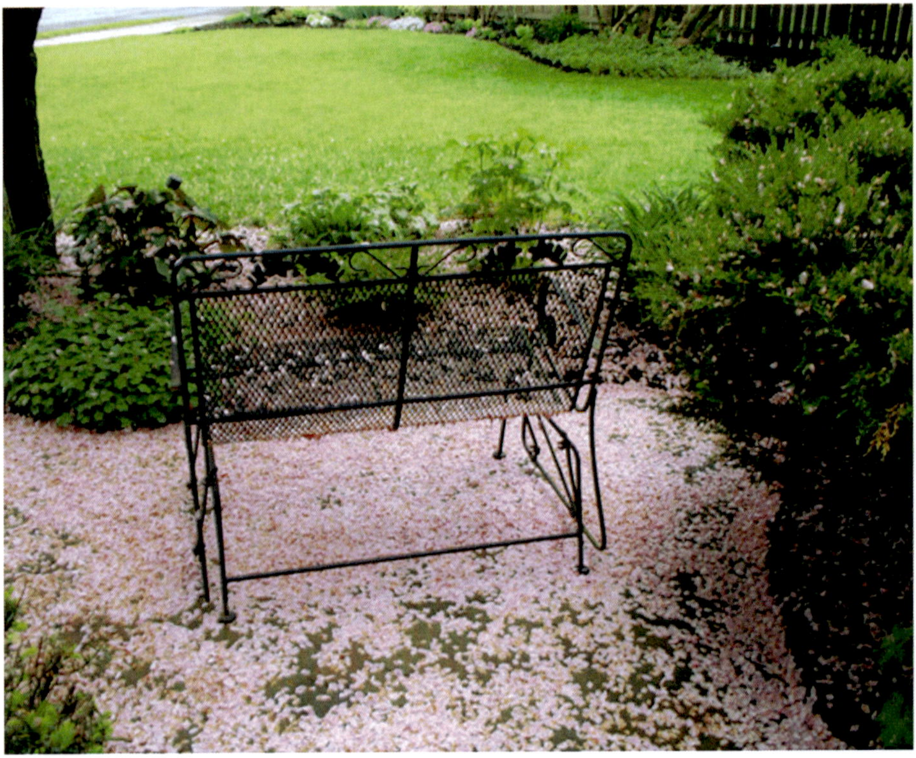

Ashok Kumar Malhotra

Chapter 77

Balance

The Tao's working in the world is similar to the bending of a bow.
The top is made lower and the bottom is made higher.
If the string is short, it is made larger
and if it is large, it is made shorter.
Thus through making these adjustments,
the Tao keeps the balance.
It takes from those who have too much
and gives to those who have too little.
The man of Tao is generous in giving
and asks nothing in return.
He achieves without asking for recognition.
He desires nothing and everything comes to him.

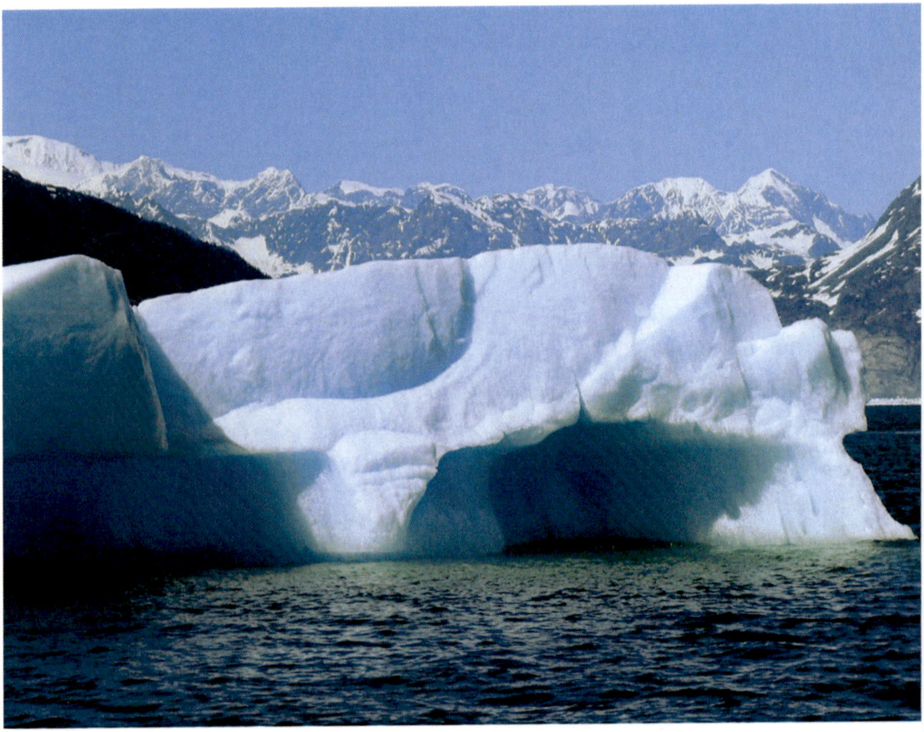

Wisdom of the Tao Te Ching

Chapter 78

Paradoxical Truth

Though water is softer and yielding than everything,
it overcomes the hardest and strongest.
The weak conquers the strong
and the soft conquers the hard.
Though it is an obvious truth,
yet no one puts it into practice.
The wise man feels the suffering of others
and thus is their savior.
He takes upon himself the burden of the world
and thus is kingly.
Though this is the truth, it appears to be paradoxical.

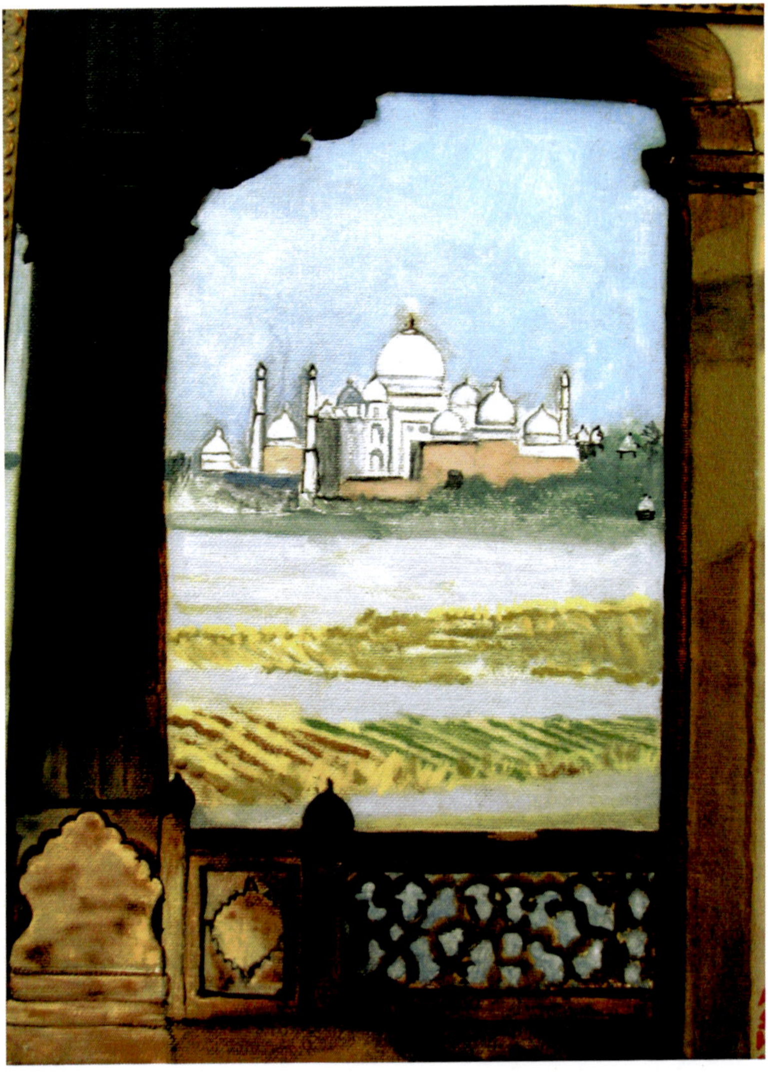

Chapter 79

Good Men

Even when the great conflict is resolved, some of it remains.
How does one handle this?
A wise man accepts his end of the bargain without blaming the other party.
A man of the Tao sticks to his part of the deal
whereas the man without the Tao wants the other to stick to the deal.
Though the Tao favors no one yet it resides in the heart of good men.

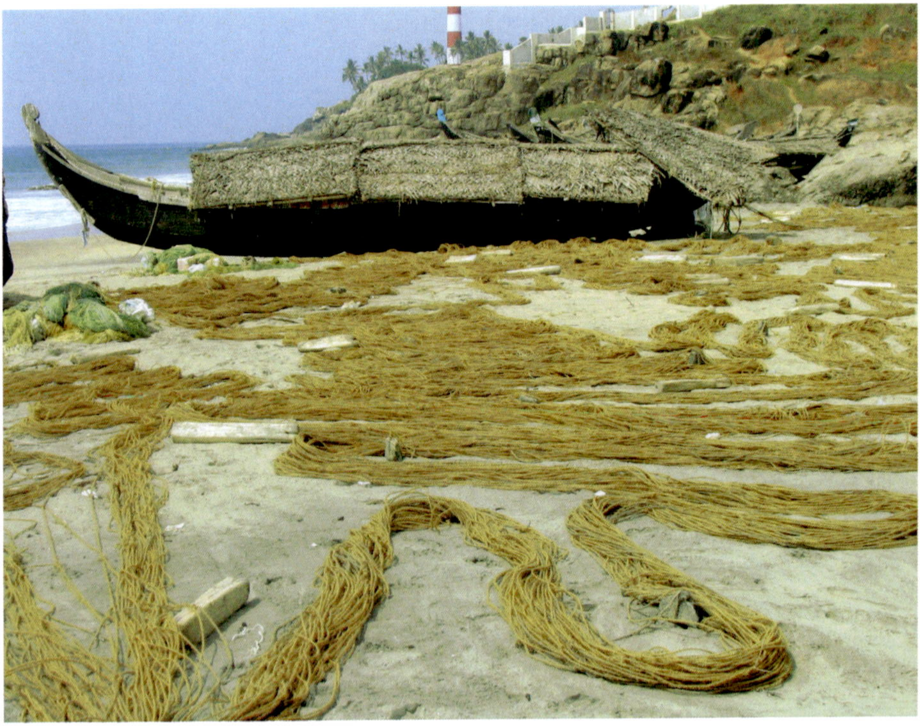

Wisdom of the Tao Te Ching

Chapter 80

Ideal Life

What is the ideal life for the people of a small country?
Though there might be machines to do the work,
they prefer to use their own hands.
They take life and death seriously
without journeying far from their homes.
They might have ships and carts
without ever putting them to use.
They might have arms and ammunition
without ever exhibiting them.
They are content with tying their ropes,
enjoying their food,
wearing nice clothes,
spending time with their children and family,
enjoying their homes,
and taking pleasure in their daily chores.
They might hear the neighbor's barking dogs
and crowing roosters,
but decide to stay home till their dying day
without ever visiting another land.

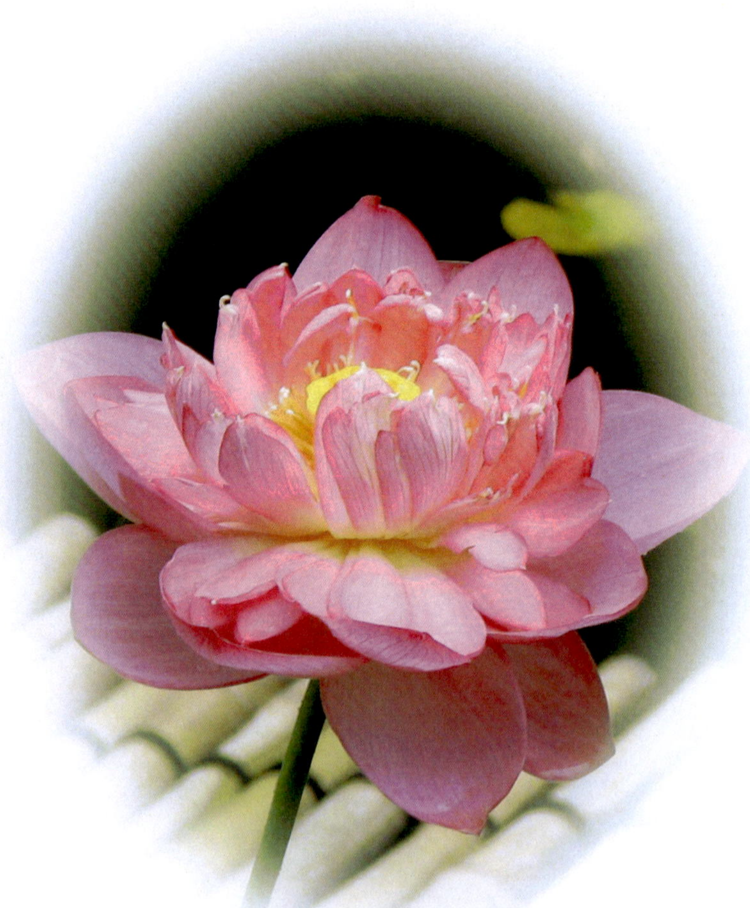

Ashok Kumar Malhotra

Chapter 81

Pure Action

Honest words are not elegant.
Elegant words are not honest.
A good man does not argue.
One who argues is not good.
A wise man is not filled with all knowledge.
One who is filled with knowledge is not wise.
A sage dispossesses himself by giving to others.
The more he does for others, the more they do for him.
The more he gives to others, the more wealth flows toward him.
Thus, Tao gives without asking anything in return
and the sage performs pure action without claiming.

AFTERWORD

Reflections on the Tao of Life, Love, and Death

The themes of living a fulfilled life, of experiencing romantic love, and of dying a dignified death have been discussed at great length by various writers of the past and the present. Though different religious-philosophical traditions have delved into these issues, Lao Tzu and Chuang Tzu, the two founding fathers of Taoism, have provided rich insight into these subjects. In the West, philosophy as a logical system offers a theoretical understanding of life, but is unable to provide practical guidance to the living of an actual life. In this regard, Taoism has been singular, unique, and assertive. Lin Yutang, a famous Chinese scholar, highlights this distinctiveness by saying that Taoism is not just a system of philosophy in China but a way of cultural life touching every aspect from life to death, from poetry to painting, and from philosophy to theology. It is deeply imbedded in the Chinese psyche which manifests itself in the physical, emotional and mental self thus becoming a fundamental trait of Chinese thinking and living.

Both Lao Tzu and Chuang Tzu were philosophers and not professors of philosophy. Their interest did not lay in offering analytical arguments to present and defend their philosophical positions but in living a fulfilled life here and now. Arguments and analysis for them were appropriate when one was explaining someone else's views to students but they were useless as a guide to living. A professor of philosophy might have all the analytical skills to defend or reject a position but might never put these insights into practice. In contrast, a philosopher is one who practices what he preaches. Like the Buddha and Socrates, both Lao Tzu and Chuang Tzu believed that the way they lived their daily lives indicated how their philosophies were put to practice. By slightly modifying the contemporary slang, we could say that both Lao Tzu and Chuang Tzu not only talked, but "walked their talk." The living of their daily life became their message. Since the lives of Lao Tzu and Chuang Tzu exemplified the basic principles of the Taoist's philosophy, their vision of life became deeply embedded into the psyche of the Chinese and is clearly displayed in the Chinese approach to art, literature, poetry, society, and the living of life.

Here a description of some of the Taoist tenets relating to love, life and death as expressed in the *Tao Te Ching* and *Chuang Tzu* will be provided. These principles are not stated as constituting an ideal kind of existence but for the living of an authentic life, the experiencing of an actual romance and the preparing for a dignified death. Since the concept of the *Tao* is central to Taoism, a discussion of the themes of life, love, and death within the context of the nature of the *Tao* is essential to the understanding of the Taoist philosophy.

Wisdom of the Tao Te Ching

The Tao of Life

In the *Tao Te Ching*, Lao Tzu points out that the ultimate reality is the unmanifest *Tao*. Beyond name and form, it is ineffable. Though the *Tao* is eternal and uncreated, it is the creative source of all that exists. Like the mystic mother, it gives birth to everything, resides in everything, and is readily available to nourish anyone. When an aspect of the unmanifest *Tao* becomes manifest, the diversity of things is born. Each created being carries within it the signature of the parent *Tao*. This distinguishing mark of the *Tao* called the *Te* is present in each animal and human being as their nature or natural ability. The goal of life is to experience this natural ability in every thought, act and deed. A happy, contented, and fulfilled life consists of getting in touch with one's *Te* and conducting one's entire life in tune with its rhythm. When one goes against one's natural ability, one suffers. To avoid physical, psychological, and spiritual suffering, Lao Tzu recommends living one's life in conformity with the flow of the *Tao*. Since nature is the foremost educator, one should live a life by taking delight in it, by contemplating it, and by blending with the cosmic flux.

Lao Tzu asserts that nature is an open book imbued with wisdom. Each of its creations has a story to tell. One can learn profound lessons from the flight of birds, the murmuring sound of water, the morning dew, and the rays of the sun. The earth and the sun are compassionate towards every created being. They shower their generosity by giving everything without asking anything in return. By contemplating nature and natural processes, one can gain the highest wisdom about the mysterious Tao. A life patterned on the model of a child, for whom every sound, taste, smell and touch is an adventure and every step a new beginning, is most conductive to capturing the practical wisdom made available to us by nature.

While complementing the naturalistic views of Lao Tzu, Chuang Tzu emphasizes inwardness. For him, freedom and happiness do not dwell in the artifacts of civilization but in the inner recesses of one's being because here resides the *Te,* the wonderful contribution of the *Tao* to humanity. We are born to experience this highest of gifts by taking an inward journey. But most of us are mislead into believing that happiness and contentment lie in the external world of human creation. We spend our lives pursuing and chasing after goals set by others and look for contentment in the caves, the forests or the ancient and modern books of the scholars. The more we look for freedom and happiness in these strange and secret places the less we will find them. The artificial world of values and goals created by the selfish interests of human beings, is far removed from providing the contentment one seeks. The secret of total freedom and happiness lies in experiencing the flow of the *Tao* within one's being. Chuang Tzu offers a simple maxim for guidance: "if you want to gain wisdom about the universe explore your own home first."

Is there a special way which when adopted can make

Wisdom of the Tao Te Ching

possible the experience of the *Tao*? Do Lao Tzu and Chuang Tzu suggest a step by step procedure to achieve this goal? Though both of them firmly believe that happiness is within a person's grasp if one lives a certain kind of life, they are equally adamant in suggesting any special method to achieve it. Chuang Tzu openly rejects any deliberate attempt at the cultivation of inwardness. No planned course of action is suitable to attain refinement of inner life. Even if such a method is found it will be unsuccessful because it will limit itself to finding contentment in a specific deed or attitude when in actuality happiness is found everywhere and available to anyone at any time.

Though Lao Tzu and Chuang Tzu reject the suitability of any specific method to the achieving of happiness, both of them assign utmost importance to the contemplation of the *Tao*. Lao Tzu asserts in unambiguous terms that happiness can be achieved by going out into nature where one sees, hears, tastes, smells, touches, and feels the flow of the *Tao* in all of its created forms. The nature of the universe is basically very simple. Every created being is an accessible book with a wonderful message. When we approach nature with an open mind and an accepting heart it will reveal its deep secrets to us. But if you go to it with a contrived method, access to its mystery will be denied for ever.

On the other hand, Chuang Tzu emphasizes the importance of the inward journey, where one digs deeper into the core of one's being. In place of contemplating nature and its created forms, one makes one's own mind as the subject of experience. One delves into the mystery of one's consciousness by crossing the waves of sensations, feelings, emotions, passions, images, words, values, and ideas and by plunging into the core of one's being where the *Tao* dwells. In the case of Lao Tzu, nature is willing to unravel its secrets when approached with the innocence and playfulness of a child. While seeing, hearing, tasting, touching, smelling and feeling nature, one should take delight in it as if it were one's first time. Like a pioneer, when one feels the excitement of discovery and the elation of being touched by the diverse aspects of nature, one is drawn closer to experience of the flow of the *Tao*. While agreeing with Lao Tzu about his childlike approach to nature that carries no previous conceptual baggage, Chuang Tzu offers the unique life style of idleness and forgetfulness of the surrounding world. When one discards one's ego and gets away from its trappings of desires and allurement, one opens oneself up to the experience of one's inner nature, which is the *Te*, a unique gift from the *Tao*. In this comprehension dwells contentment and fulfilment.

The Tao of Love

Both Lao Tzu and Chuang Tzu develop their views on love and death in conjunction with the living of a happy and contented life here and now. There are a number of passages in the *Tao Te Ching* and the *Chuang Tzu* that describe the nature of love and death in relation to the nature of the *Tao*. According to Lao Tzu and Chuang Tzu,

Wisdom of the Tao Te Ching

when one grasps the correct meaning of love and death, one adds a special flavor to the definition of living a joyful life. If the mystery of love is comprehended, one will be able to experience the flow of the *Tao* in every act of love, and if the significance of death is understood, one will be eternally fulfilled.

When Lao Tzu describes love, it is in the context of the *Tao*. Like the *Tao*, love is something dynamic and not static. It means caring, giving, and leading without imposing one's will on the other. Love expresses itself through the acts of nourishing, replenishing, respecting, and letting the other be free. Moreover, love consists of seeing the other person as one's self, letting the other be oneself, loving the other as oneself, and caring for the other as if one were that person. Moreover, love means fulfilling one's companion rather than seeking this companion for one's own fulfillment. Love for Lao Tzu is like a well which is used but is never used up. Similar to the *Tao*, love is like an inexhaustible reservoir that offers infinite possibilities. The more you drink from it, the more you want others to drink from it. Not only you are fulfilled by it, you share this contentment with others.

Many thinkers of the twentieth century have incorporated Lao Tzu's views on love in their own writings. This influence is clearly evident in the works of Rabindranath Tagore, a great poet and philosopher of India. Tagore's famous work, *Gitanjali*, which was responsible for earning him the Noble Prize for Literature in 1913, clearly indicates that it was influenced by Lao Tzu's views on love and death. Tagore believes that love and death are alike at their core. In love, a lover merges one's ego into that of the beloved. By uniting one's self with that of the beloved, the lover becomes the other and thus experiences the human self which is greater than their unique limited egos. Similarly, in death one's limited self merges into the universal self more like a drop of rain which takes a plunge into the ocean and becomes the ocean.

The Tao of Relationships by Ray Grigg develops the Taoist philosophy of love in a significant way. Grigg elevates lovers to the level of sages because he thinks that the love between a man and a woman is comparable to the love between a sage and the *Tao*. He holds that the loving that is between lovers is the model for all nature. Everything else follows its example.

The *Tao* and love have similar natures. Neither of them is an object which could be studied or defined. Rather they are processes to be experienced and emulated. Being beyond all definition and explanation, both can be felt, revered, and enjoyed. According to Grigg, though we cannot conceptualize the *Tao* yet everything in nature follows its directive with precision whether they are the rivers that flow down valleys or the seeds that sprout or the male being attracted by the female or the night that is enamored by the day and is greeted by the day again next morning. The *Tao* is the creative substance and the cement of everything. It is the universal motion and the urge that keeps all objects and beings together. While comparing love to the *Tao*, Grigg points out that the attraction that man has for the woman or the root's symbiotic connection to the flower, or the leaf's to its soil, and the breath to wind is not contrived but due to the *Tao*. Man and woman, air and mist, rain and river, mountain and valley, they come together because of the mysterious connection to the *Tao*. They are part of the inscrutable reality. It is through loving that the profoundness of the *Tao* can be experienced and assimilated.

How can one understand and inculcate this process of loving into one's daily life? Grigg offers some suggestions from the *Tao Te Ching*.

The entire universe is born out of the inseparable and intimate romance between the unmanifest and manifest *Tao*. The sage who is part of the manifest experiences this romance by modeling one's own life after it. When properly understood, the universe is the dance of the polar interaction of the forces of *yin* and *yang*. Man and woman are the embodiment of these universal impulses. Love between man and woman reveals the same harmony that exists between the sage and the universe. In Grigg's words, man and woman enact physically and emotionally the union between *yin* and *yang*. Man is the outstanding whereas the woman is the instanding. They are incomplete without the other and need each other. Their physical and emotional togetherness helps them transcend their separateness. They are created to fill the other's emptiness and by so doing they fulfill each other. Without the other, they will be incomplete. But by being together, the emptiness that seeks fulfillment and the fulness that craves emptiness to empty itself so that it could be fulfilled are following the natural course of the apparent separateness and indissoluble connection of the yin and yang. In loving, one reveals oneself as separate and yet intimately connected to the fabric of the whole which is the *Tao*.

The Tao of Death

Similar to the themes of life and love, the Taoists discuss the subject of death in connection with the *Tao* by raising some crucial questions: What is death and how is it related to the Tao? How should one accept death? What is the significance of death? Why does one try to escape from it? Lao Tzu and Chuang Tzu discuss these questions in their respective works.

In the *Tao Te Ching*, Lao Tzu points out that whosoever is involved in the contemplation of the *Tao* will grasp the nature and significance of both life and death. Such a person can deal with whatever life offers and is ready when death visits. By taking repose in the *Tao* and by "going with the flow," a person who holds back nothing from life looks forward to death like a person who after a day's hard work looks forward to a deep sleep. In Lao Tzu's words, the sage lets himself be assimilated by the flow of natural events. He grasps the inevitability of death and holds on to nothing. His mind is cleansed of attachment and his

Wisdom of the Tao Te Ching

body resists nothing. He acts effortlessly and lets the flow of life to take its natural course. He lives each day fully immersed in the *Tao* and when death knocks at his door, he is ready to embrace it without repugnance. Chuang Tzu, who finds death to be a revelation of the *Tao*, regards it to be the most significant link that opens a door to the eternal mystery of the creative process. He asserts that death is to be revered, joyfully embraced and celebrated.

Chuang Tzu believes that there is a time for everything. Nature is an unfolding cosmic drama of sequence of events. As in nature, spring is followed by summer, autumn and winter, so in human life, birth is followed by youth, old age and death. When one grasps this natural flow of events and learns to abide by this inevitability, one frees oneself from the clutches of sorrow and unhappiness and attains peace, serenity and tranquility of mind.

How can one prepare to die a dignified death? Most of us have been conditioned to view death as a horrifying event. The mere thought of it sends shivers through every part of our being. Chuang Tzu relates the fear of death to three factors. First, we are ignorant about the natural forces responsible for the creation and destruction of life; second, we fail to grasp the intimate link between life and death; and third, we are deeply attached to our ego. In order to get rid of the fear of death, we need to understand the unique relationship between the unmanifest and the manifest *Tao*. The unmanifest, which is eternally present, is the parent of the manifest world of objects, animals and human beings. Before our birth, we were part of the formless *Tao*, after birth we become part of the formed *Tao* and on death we merge back into the formless *Tao*. At no time our connection to the *Tao* is broken. Birth and death are precious links among a series of events arranged in the manifest *Tao*. To be born means leaving the unformed to become the formed and death means leaving the formed to merge back into the unformed. When one grasps this unique connection, one loses the fear of death. Moreover, Chuang Tzu believes that understanding the nature of death in this fashion is rewarding in the following ways: first death is a wonderful opportunity bestowed upon us to bring all our restlessness and suffering to a standstill; second death provides a glimpse into eternity, third, death is the culmination and fulfillment of life, and fourth, at the time of death, when the ego is eliminated, suffering and sorrow cease and restfulness is achieved. Thus by grasping the true nature of the *Tao* and its inevitable connection to life and death, one can enhance the joy of life and diminish the fear of death.

Examples abound in the religious-philosophical traditions of both the East and the West regarding the art of dying. The views of the Taoists on death parallel those of Socrates in the West and Tagore in the East.

The life and death of Socrates is an excellent example in the West of living a dignified life and dying a dignified death. Socrates was charged by the Athenian jury with heresy and corrupting the youth and was condemned to

Wisdom of the Tao Te Ching

death. When he was asked if he was afraid of dying, his response was no. He believed that since the training in philosophy was an excellent preparation for a dignified death, a true philosopher practiced death all the time. Moreover, he looked upon death either as an eternal dreamless sleep or as the migration of the soul from one realm to another. In the first case, as after a day's hard work a person looked forward to a night of dreamless sleep so did a philosopher entertained the oncoming death without fear. As a seeker of truth, a philosopher believed that truth could be discovered only when one freed the soul from the clutches of both the material body and the ego. A philosopher must train oneself to transcend these two hindrances in order to gain wisdom. The dawning of wisdom prepares one for accepting death with dignity. Therefore, Socrates who was never terrified of death looked forward to it with a sense of relief.

In the East, Rabindranath Tagore, in his famous poem, Gitanjali, revealed his indebtedness to the Taoist views on love and death. This poem appeared to be a 20th century rendering of the *Tao Te Ching* in a poetic form as imagined by the artist-sage of India. In this important work, Tagore offered a romantic vision of anticipating death with open arms.

Tagore believed that like the Tao the ultimate source of everything was the inscrutable one. Though all names and forms were born from it, it remained nameless behind its own creation. Each life was a wonderful gift bestowed by this inscrutable maker who became the mother at the occasion of one's birth and the nurturing father that enchanted the newly born with colors and shapes as well as flowers and clouds. Tagore's poetic eye looked at the entire universe as a tapestry of colors and forms spread out and nourished by this inscrutable artist who remained hidden. Since everything was carefully crafted by the artist of the universe, death was regarded as a finale of the life's symphony. Moreover, death was conceived as a natural progression of life in conformity with nature's unique way. For Tagore, since death was the culmination of life where the life's long journey was completed, one should greet it with a joyous embrace.

Tagore perceived his own death as the most important guest who would to be served with one's own life: its joys and sorrows, accomplishments and riches, feelings and dealings as well as loves and possessions. Tagore's poetic fancy reaches its Zenith when he elevated the status of death to that of a true lover whose one glance would take away everything in an instant i.e. whatever used to be "his" would be "hers now." Furthermore, Tagore likened death to a wedding ceremony where the bride who had been eagerly waiting was finally going to be united with her bridegroom. Since death was like the union of the lost ray of light with the sun, its source or like the rain drop waiting to be assimilated into the big ocean, its source and final abode, one should anticipate death with fearlessness and submit to it with total acceptance.

Wisdom of the Tao Te Ching

Tagore entertained his own death as a friend – an event of cosmic proportion. He regarded his short life on earth as a free gift where he got more than he could give back. Furthermore, death for Tagore was not an end but a new beginning – the continuation of life eternal. Similar to Chuang Tzu, death invoked no fear or resentment in Tagore. It was rather an occasion to make a contented move in the direction of something higher which would complete his transient journey on this earth. Finally, like the Taoists, Tagore looked forward to this fulfillment of life by embracing his own death with joy unalloyed.

BIBLIOGRAPHY

Roger Ames, *The Art of Rulership: A Study in Ancient Chinese Political Thought*. Honolulu: University of Hawaii Press, 1983.

Stephen Addiss and Stanley Lombardo, tr., *Tao Te Ching*. Indianapolis: Hackett Publishing Co., 1993.

Usharbudh Arya. *Meditation and the Art of Dying*. Honesdale: The Himalayan International Institute, 1985.

Archie J. Bahm, *Tao The King By Lao Tzu: Interpreted as Nature and Intelligence*. Albuquerque: World Books, 1986.

Witter Bynner, tr., *The Way of Life According to Lao Tzu*. New York: Capricorn Books, 1944.

Wing-tsit Chan, *A Source Book in Chinese Philosophy*. Princeton: Princeton University Press, 1963.

Hurlee, G. Creel, *Chinese Thought from Confucius to Mao Tse-tung*. Chicago: University of Chicago Press, 1953.

William Theodore De Bary, et al., *Sources of Chinese Traditions*. New York: Columbia University Press, 1960.

Gia-Fu Feng and Jane English, *Tao Te Ching*. New York: Vintage Books: 1972.

Herbert Fingarette, *Confucius: The Secular as Sacred*. New York: Harper and Row, 1972.

Wisdom of the Tao Te Ching

A. C. Graham, *Disputers of Tao: Philosophical Arguments in Ancient China*. La Salle, Ill. Open Court, 1989.

Erich Fromm. *The Art of Loving*. New York: Harper Collins, 1956.

Ray Grigg. *The Tao of Relationship*. New York: Bantam Books, 1989.

Chad Hansen, *A Daoist Theory Of Chinese Thought: A Philosophical Interpretation*. New York: Oxford University Press, 1992.

Robert Henricks, *Lao Tzu: Tao Te Ching: A New Translation Based on the Recently Discovered Ma-wang-tui Texts*. New York: Ballantine, 1989.

Philip J. Ivanhoe, *The Daodeching of Laozi*. New York: Seven Bridges Press, 2002.

John M. Koller, *Asian Philosophies*. New Jersey: Prentice Hall, 2002.

Michael LaFargue, *The Tao of the Tao Te Ching: A Translation And Commentary*. Albany: State University of New York Press, 1992.

Victor H. Mair, *Tao Te Ching: The Classic Book of Integrity And The Way*. New York: Bantam Books, 1990.

Stephen Mitchell, *Tao Te Ching: A New Version, with Foreword and Notes.* New York: Harper Collins Publishers, 1988.

Henry Rosemont, *Chinese Texts and Philosophical Contexts: Essays Dedicated to Angus C. Graham, Vol. I.* Chicago: Open Court Publishing Company, 1992.

Benjamin Schwartz, *The World of Thought in Ancient China.* Cambridge, Mass.: Harvard University Press, 1985.

Douglas Shrader and Ashok Malhotra, *Pathways to Philosophy: A Multidisciplinary Approach.* New Jersey: Prentice Hall, 1996.

Rabindranath Tagore. *Gitanjali.* New Delhi: Macmillan India Limited, 1995.

Arthur Waley. *Three Ways of Thought in Ancient China.* New York: Doubleday Anchor, 1956.

Fung Yu-Lan, *A Short History of Chinese Philosophy.* New York: MacMillan Publishing Co., 1948.

Lin Yutang, Ed.,*The Wisdom of China and India.* New York: The Modern Library, 1952.